MANAGING
CONTRACTED
SERVICES IN THE
NONPROFIT AGENCY

MANAGING CONTRACTED SERVICES IN THE NONPROFIT AGENCY

Administrative, Ethical, and Political Issues

Susan R. Bernstein

Foreword by **Roger A. Lohmann**

TEMPLE UNIVERSITY PRESS
Philadelphia

Temple University Press, Philadelphia 19122
Copyright © 1991 by Temple University. All rights reserved
Published 1991
Printed in the United States of America

The paper used in this publication meets the minimum
requirements of American National Standard for Information
Sciences—Permanence of Paper for Printed Library Materials,
ANSI Z39.48-1984 ∞

Library of Congress Cataloging-in-Publication Data
Bernstein, Susan R., 1948–
    Managing contracted services in the nonprofit agency :
administrative, ethical, and political issues / Susan R. Bernstein ;
foreword by Roger A. Lohmann.
        p. cm.
    ISBN 0-87722-808-6 (alk. paper).
    1. Human services—United States—Contracting out.   2. Human
services—United States—Management.   3. Corporations,
Nonprofit—United States—Management.   I. Title.
HV91.B44   1991
361'0068—dc20   91-270
                                                                          CIP

CONTENTS

FOREWORD

Roger A. Lohmann

There has been an upsurge of research and scholarly interest in social administration since the mid-1970s. The general outlines are plain to see: Course offerings expanded and enrollments increased in specialized concentrations in the traditional professional programs of social work, public health, and public administration. Specialized journals devoted to social work administration, mental health administration, and human services administration made their appearance. Books on esoteric management topics like financial management, budgeting, personnel, and cost studies appeared alongside those on the classic subjects of fund raising and accounting. More than a dozen general administration textbooks have been published in the last decade.

This upsurge of interest in social administration can be taken as a sign that there is a sense of trouble in and about agency executive suites. Initially that sense may have been a by-product of the chaos engendered by big infusions of cash into social services in the late 1960s and through the mid-1970s and the startup of the many new agencies created to receive that cash. A large cadre of instant administrators was cashiered in that period. Such opportunity crises were all too quickly replaced, however, by a sense of perpetual crisis and "cutback management" as by-products of the conservative social revolution of the late 1970s and 1980s. Entirely new service delivery systems were built on soft money in the form of grants. These same systems allegedly became "more businesslike" with the advent of performance contracting. This latter move institutionalized instability and uncertainty and contributed to an entirely new class of what Dennis Young has called "nonprofit entrepreneurs."

The general social work response to these developments has been only minimal interest. Financial and economic questions are conceded to be critically important, but the actual amount of day-to-day scholarly interest in this area remains limited, in part because social workers and other human service professionals are not particularly interested in, or proficient at, the esoterics of human service finance. Most work done in this area fits comfortably within the long tradition of administrators' reporting their own experiences or the quantitative research paradigms of accounting, economics, or management theory. It has limited appeal to the general social work audience.

This book is different. Susan Bernstein brings a major new voice—and an entirely new and fresh research strategy—to the study of the management of human services. By talking with a large number of participants in the contract services system and letting them report their experiences in their own words rather than synthesizing them into survey statistics, she has assembled a unique and disturbing picture of an administrative system at war with itself.

Simply because this study was done in New York City, there may be those willing to discount the disturbing picture it paints. After all, that New York is unmanageable is a foregone conclusion in many quarters today. Ignoring Bernstein's work, however, on this or any other basis would be a big mistake. The very first thing that struck me about the accounts reported in this book is how they ring true to experience elsewhere. Like all good qualitative research, Bernstein's account has the universality and dramatic tension of a novel. The scale of operations reported in this study may be uniquely New York City, but the underlying sense of tension of those working in this system will be all too familiar to practitioners working with contract services in the most remote rural settings: Reasonable professionals (mostly women and MSWs) are pictured coping in the best ways they know how with what they suspect is an insane system.

In this work, Bernstein is consistently a dispassionate observer and reporter, the objective social scientist, scrupulously avoiding polemics and merely reporting and bringing order to the comments of her interview subjects. She demonstrates a real command of her subject and genuine mastery of a medium—the qualitative research study—which has proven to be a very difficult one for social work research.

Qualitative methods are intuitively appealing to person-oriented social workers turned researchers. And as Mary Jo Deegan has shown in her 1988 study *Jane Addams and the Men of the Chicago School, 1892–1918* (New Brunswick, N.J.: Transaction Books), there is a strong historical link between social workers involved in the settlement movement and the founders of symbolic interaction, which may be the most consistent and deeply rooted theoretical position supporting qualitative methods in the social sciences. On the other hand, few in social work have been able to master the difficult and demanding tasks of qualitative research without letting their instincts to advise, moralize, and recommend changes get in the way.

Because of the relative recency of interest in social administration, a large body of research findings has not been built up. Most of the textbooks, in fact, borrow heavily from research done in the sociology of organizations, business management, or public administration. Susan Bernstein's study is equally significant on two counts: It joins the small but growing body of professional literature on the implications of the contracted services system as the system is evolving. It stands alone in that literature (and in the social administration literature generally) in its use of qualitative methodology.

ACKNOWLEDGMENTS

In acknowledging the assistance of the government monitor of her contracted service, a manager interviewed for this study said, "I don't know what I would have done really. The budget—my Lord, I didn't know what I would do. But somehow we got it together." Those who were with me in getting this book together were many, and my gratitude to them is profound.

The anonymous managers, who entrusted me with their experiences and perspectives, provided both the substance and soul of the research. Their voices were a continuing source of inspiration: Their individuality, compassion, and commitment resonate in their words. I hope they feel the findings do justice to their story, to the reality and complexity of their jobs.

Irwin Epstein, over the years of the study's gestation, was an extraordinary mentor. His contributions to the conceptualization, evolution, and completion of the research, as well as its intellectual stimulation and satisfaction, were pivotal.

Robert Salmon, Simon Slavin, and Harold Weissman were key supporters. Their respective interests in the operational, philosophical/historical, and universal dimensions of contracting extended my own.

The computer made the study's depth possible. Carlos Dragovich, Tom Givler, Tony Ferrigno, and David Spencer provided a range of indispensable technical direction. The writing was improved markedly by the guidance of Roger Lohmann, Michael

Ames, and Deborah Stuart. Joe Thom and Janette Handley made the production of the manuscript enjoyable.

At every stage, in their own special ways, Fred Ephraim, Maryann Lienhard, and Dina Pruzansky provided invaluable assistance and support.

Finally, my husband, Josh Pruzansky, was there for me through all the years on which this kind of effort rests. But for his encouragement and sustenance, the book would not have happened.

To these people, especially, and to the many others whose interest in this work was so heartening, I convey my appreciation and acknowledge my indebtedness. Without them, "I don't know what I would have done really."

MANAGING CONTRACTED SERVICES IN THE NONPROFIT AGENCY

C H A P T E R   O N E

THE WORLD OF NONPROFIT AGENCY MANAGERS

To reconcile their constituents' simultaneous beliefs in less and in more governmental involvement, legislators in the United States have increasingly used contracting.[1] They find people are more accepting of "government funding and standard setting if nongovernmental organizations deliver the public goods and services."[2] This reconciliation strategy has inherent conflicts, however, which have created a "philosophical and administrative mess"[3] that is unlikely to be cleaned up because many groups have vested interests in its maintenance.[4] This "mess" is characterized by complex questions of accountability.

Social welfare policies in the United States vary significantly by community.[5] Without national policy implemented in "a public baseline system of services that has clarity about its role, function, and priorities," it has been suggested that contracting makes no sense, that it "is an upside down problem that offers no clues about how to set things right."[6] Two documented manifestations of this "upside down problem" are the control of government purchasers by service providers and the segregated, inequitable distribution of services.[7]

For example, researchers for a taxpayers' organization concluded that their state has inadequate fiscal and program control over its service system because the system is " 'provider dominated.' " This "situation," they assert, " 'is self-perpetuating' because providers have become such an important part of the service system that [state] agencies cannot run their programs without them." Thus, the state agencies "fear losing" the providers.[8] In the New York City child welfare system, similar concerns about providers' control over services have been raised.[9]

There is evidence that contracting results in the poorest being least served. Nonprofit agencies, which provide more government-funded services than does the government itself, help less-needy clients with better treatment, possibly because they also have nongovernmental resources.[10] Also, as government funding is reduced, services to the poor are disproportionately cut because agencies serving them cannot recoup funding losses with fees for service or with contributions.[11]

Quality control in human service organizations is inherently problematic because of the elusive program and treatment goals of these organizations and their limited resources and inexact technologies.[12] These problems are exacerbated when contracts are involved because it is so difficult to develop valid, realistic contractual requirements sufficient to achieve accountability but not so burdensome that they result in more compliance activity than service.[13] When contracting occurs among different governmental levels, increased political influences and constraints complicate quality control.[14] When contracting occurs between one or more levels of government (federal, state, and local) and nonprofit or for-profit agencies, or a combination of the two, this complexity has staggering implications for accountability.[15]

While these questions of accountability are somewhat abstract, the related operational problems for nonprofit agency managers are quite concrete.[16] Consistently reported to be most significant are financial problems, including delays in reimbursement, insufficient reimbursement, and restrictions on budget modifications.[17] Profuse, often conflicting, contract requirements are costly and problematic to manage.[18]

The contracting process itself is another serious problem. Short submission time for proposals, inadequately trained government staff and their frequent turnover, time gaps before renewals, and award and approval delays are major difficulties.[19] Contracting typically occurs on an annual cycle, often with multiple agencies having myriad purposes, people, and regulations. For managers, the complexity and irrationality of the process is vexing.[20]

The few studies that have been made of the management of contracted services conclude that many of the problems are not amenable to an individual nonprofit agency's or administrator's control. Changes in the contracting system, by joint effort of nonprofit agencies and government, are recommended.[21] However, neither how such joint effort might be initiated and sustained nor what would be required for success is addressed.[22]

The research and practice literature, however, does suggest some ways for nonprofit agency administrators to manage contracting problems. For anticipating and preventing problems, managers are offered general advice corresponding to basic management principles and some specific hints, for example, about how to avoid underpayment and reimbursement delays.[23] Specific strategies and a worksheet for managing predictable relationship problems with funding agencies are recommended.[24] One researcher, after suggesting that managers diversify funding sources, write ambiguous funding proposals, and develop endowments to cope with the "dilemmas of funding," concludes that there are "no easy answers" and urges managers "to be aware enough to look gift horses in the mouth and to anticipate and be prepared for it when they buck."[25]

Another researcher offers advice about how to change a funding agency's position through such political strategies as the use of cooperation/cooptation techniques to maximize communication and ensure that disagreements are handled amicably. If conflicts do arise, negotiation/bargaining and mediation/appeal are proposed as strategies to help resolve them.[26]

To ensure that they meet regulatory requirements, some nonprofit agencies have created a compliance coordinator position or function. The coordinator's responsibility is "to promote the link between compliance and the provision of quality care" and prevent the displacement of the goals of the latter by those of the former. To do so, specific suggestions have been made.[27]

Although agency administrators often manipulate budgets and "adjust" service statistics to meet the requirements of a funding source or the needs of clients, to get done what has to be done in the agency, or to effect an acceptable financial statement, such manipulation is nowhere explicitly recommended as a management approach or acknowledged directly as a contract management strategy.[28] Curiously, existing research offers little explanation of how administrators have been able to manage budgets and programs despite all the identified problems and the need for systemic solutions. The authors of one report allude, only in their conclusions, with no documentation elsewhere, to what might be the explanation. In recommending that funding agencies set a uniform percentage for indirect costs, they speculate that this will "mitigate the need to 'manipulate' budget lines in order to make ends meet."[29] Another researcher cites a "frequent" kind of budget manipulation: "Staff from [contracted] programs are used to perform general tasks for the agency."[30] Manipulation of service statistics can take a number of forms.

- reporting visits or services rendered, as required by the contract, when fewer occurred than are recorded;
- reporting services (or clients) as new, which (or who) were actually being provided (or served) before the current funding;
- reporting services as provided under one source of funding when they were actually provided through another source;
- reporting as eligible for services clients who are only so by the most imaginative interpretation of eligibility criteria; and
- creative writing about activities that actually occurred so that they seem to match the provisions of the contract; however, what actually was done has little to do with the intent of the funding agency.

A few graphic examples of these kinds of manipulation have been recorded.[31]

The voluminous literature on management contains much lofty advice about what managers should do. However, the complex reality of organizational life makes successful management exceptionally arduous and presents profound methodological problems for finding out what managers actually do.[32] Most of the early research on management sought to describe how managers spend their time.[33] A review of over a hundred studies of managerial behavior yielded ten empirically supported generalizations.

> Managers work long hours; they are busy doing a lot of things; their work is fragmented and episodes are brief; the job contains a lot of variety; managers spend the bulk of their time within their own parts of the organization;

the work is predominantly oral; managers have contact
with a variety of people (by no means all in the direct
chain of command); managers are not reflective planners;
information is the core of the job; and finally, managers
really don't have an accurate picture of how they spend
their time.[34]

Nevertheless, beyond these generalizations, it is difficult to determine how managers spend their time.[35]

Moreover, answering this descriptive question does not deal with the more essential issue of why managers do what they do. Researchers investigating managers' purposes have sought to determine what roles managers perform.[36] A seminal study concluded all managerial work is the same, involving three groups of interrelated roles (interpersonal, informational, and decisional), with varying emphasis on these roles in different jobs.[37]

Other researchers, however, were convinced that abstract managerial roles do not reflect the complex reality of managers' work and began to ask different questions and to ask in different ways to find out what managers do. "Anthropological" methods were used to identify "behavioral skills—what you do with whom and how you know when and how to do it."[38] Intensive interviews were conducted with effective managers to learn how they identify problems and decide what to do about them.[39]

The study of how managers decide what to do is now being extended to the related but more encompassing issue of how managers' thinking influences their actions: What do managers know?[40] How can they use different metaphors for organizations?[41] The objective is to have managers "become skilled in the art of 'reading' the situations that they are attempting to organize or manage—to understand the many and often paradoxical aspects of situations, and to forge appropriate actions."[42] Using ethnographic methods, other researchers have addressed the relationship between what managers know, their attitudes and perceptions, and what they do.[43]

This study used ethnographic methods to determine how nonprofit agency administrators manage the issues that arise in contracted services. Although contracting is the primary method for the financing and delivery of social welfare services in the United States and the professional literature stresses the importance of effective management of issues (or trade-offs, contingencies, exchanges, tensions), amazingly little is known about managing contracted services.[44] Through in-depth interviews with nonprofit agency managers, the study tried to capture the intense, complex reality of their work lives.[45] The findings should be replicable.[46] Hopefully, they will also "ring true" and be useful to managers.[47]

This book is for those directly involved in the broad nonprofit sector, such as managers and boards of directors, and for those with vital ties to nonprofit organizations, including federal, state, and local government policymakers and contract administrators, as well as foundation program officers. The study should also be of interest to those concerned with the trend toward privatization. For educators in social work, nonprofit, and public administration, the book offers rich material for introducing students to management as it is actually practiced.

From my review of research and my own experience, I assumed that the management of contracted services has certain generic elements unrelated to job title, field of service, type and size of agency, funding source, or type of contract. Therefore, managers were selected for diversity in each of these dimensions and from one of three categories: program directors of contracted services in multiservice agencies; executive directors of primarily smaller, single-service agencies; and compliance coordinators in child welfare and mental health agencies.

From March through July 1987, I interviewed eighteen managers from seventeen agencies in the New York City metropolitan area. Of the seventeen agencies, nine provide services primarily to families and children, three provide mental health or mental retardation services, two are multiservice agencies, one provides services to the elderly, one provides services to the homeless, and one is a hospital. Among the seventeen agencies, at least thirty-nine discrete services are provided. The annual budgets of the agencies (with the exception of the hospital-based program) range from less than $500,000 to well over $10 million. Government funds constitute from 9 percent to greater than 99 percent of the budgets. The seventeen agencies have a total of ninety-five contracts with thirty-three local, state, and federal government agencies.

Of the eighteen managers interviewed, seven are executive directors, seven are program directors, and four are responsible primarily for compliance coordination. Twelve are women; six are men. Seventeen are white; one is black. Of the eighteen, ten have their master's degree in social work; one of the ten has a doctorate in social work. Of the eight non-MSWs, five have master's degrees in other fields. Of the eighteen interviewees, eight have been in their current agency in some position twelve to seventeen years; four, for six to eight years; and six, under five years.

For clarity and consistency, certain editorial procedures were adopted. The abbreviations GFO and NPA are used for government funding organizations and nonprofit agencies, respectively. Any reference to a GFO or NPA and what they believe or how they act refers only to what a manager interviewed for this study perceives.

A GFO is defined as any body of government that funds nonprofit agencies. In many instances, the GFO for any one contract is three levels of government, because funding flows from federal to state to local government. On any governmental level, as well as between levels, a GFO for a contract typically means that more than one GFO (or governmental oversight body or a combination of the two) is involved. Only if these distinctions are relevant to the description of managers' experience are they made. Because it seems consistent with managers' perceptions, the Joint Commission on Accreditation of Healthcare Organizations (Joint Commission) is treated as if it were a GFO.[48] Although the contracts for which managers are responsible include a range of GFO funding mechanisms that could be categorized in several ways, these differences seem insignificant for an understanding of managers' experience of contracted services and so are not distinguished.[49]

An NPA is defined as an organization that does not exist to make a profit and is funded by a GFO to provide services. "NPA" is used regardless of the organization's mission or size and refers both to the entire NPA and to individual programs and departments. All NPAs and GFOs, with the exception of the Joint Commission, are referred to only as such. The term NPA coalition is frequently used to refer to an organization of NPAs that have contracts to provide the same service for the same GFO. In the few references to for-profit organizations, the abbreviation FPO is used.

References to individuals, communities, or situations, which would violate the anonymity promised interviewees for themselves and their agencies, have been disguised or deleted. None of the managers interviewed has the title of "compliance coordinator," but if that function is his or her primary responsibility, that title is used. Quotations have been edited to make them easier to read and to clarify managers' references. To ground the reader in the data, the eighteen interviewees are referred to as "managers" and their story is told in the present tense.

NOTES

1. "The United States has been characterized as a 'reluctant welfare state' because of a persistent conflict between two opposing sets of values." Harold L. Wilensky and Charles N. Lebeaux, *Industrial*

Society and Social Welfare (New York: The Free Press, 1965), p. xvii, as quoted in Ralph M. Kramer, *Voluntary Agencies in the Welfare State* (Berkeley, Calif.: University of California Press, 1981), p. 72. Kramer delineates the value conflict: "At one pole is a cluster of ideas associated with Social Darwinism, laissez-faire, individualism, free enterprise, and a distrust of government. At the other is the American creed of humanistic liberalism and a belief in progress and in governmental intervention to achieve security and equality. Related ideological dualisms in the United States are those between self-reliance and dependency, charity and justice, philanthropy and taxation, and volunteerism and bureaucracy and professionalism" (p. 72).

2. Kramer, *Voluntary Agencies*, p. 73. For a discussion of the range of arguments used for and against contracting, see Ruth Hoogland DeHoog, *Contracting Out for Human Services: Economic, Political, and Organizational Perspectives* (Albany, N.Y.: State University of New York Press, 1984), pp. 1–33.

3. Harold Orlans, "The Contract State: The Welfare State of the Professional Classes?" in Harold Orlans, ed., *Nonprofit Organizations: A Government Management Tool* (New York: Praeger, 1980), p. 122.

4. Kramer, *Voluntary Agencies*, p. 286.

5. Lester M. Salamon, James C. Musselwhite, Jr., and Carol J. De Vita, *Partners in Public Service: Government and the Nonprofit Sector in the American Welfare State* (Washington, D.C.: The Urban Institute, 1986), pp. 13–14.

6. Alfred J. Kahn, "The Impact of Purchase of Service Contracting on Social Services Delivery," in Kenneth R. Wedel, Arthur J. Katz, and Ann Weick, eds., *Social Services by Government Contract* (New York: Praeger, 1979), p. 17.

7. Ken Judge, *The Public Purchase of Social Care: British Confirmation of the American Experience* (Canterbury, England: Personal Social Services Research Unit, University of Kent at Canterbury, 1982), pp. 18–20.

8. Massachusetts Taxpayers Foundation, *Purchase of Service: Can State Government Gain Control?* (Boston, Mass., 1980), p. 51, as quoted in Bill B. Benton, Hector A. Rivera, and John R. Healy, "Perspectives/Purchase of Service: A Management Challenge for State Government," *New England Journal of Human Services* 1 (1981): 47–48.

9. Joyce Purnick, "Archdiocese Sees Foster Care Peril," *New York Times*, December 4, 1986, sec. A; Joyce Purnick, "Pact to Curb Foster Care Upsets Koch," *New York Times*, December 5, 1986, sec. B; Joyce

Purnick, "O'Connor Says He'll Drop Some Foster Care Pacts with City," *New York Times*, January 24, 1987; Joyce Purnick, "Koch Sees Diocese Foster-Care Curb," *New York Times*, February 3, 1987, sec. B; Ari L. Goldman, "Cardinal Eases Threat to Curb Foster Services," *New York Times*, March 30, 1987, sec. A; Ari L. Goldman with Michael Oreskes, "New York Foster Care: A Public–Private Battleground," *New York Times*, April 9, 1987, sec. B; Josh Barbanel, "New York Foster-Care Rules Upheld," *New York Times*, June 9, 1988, sec. B; and Suzanne Daley, "Archdiocese to Continue Foster-Care Services," *New York Times*, September 3, 1988, sec. B.
10. Bill B. Benton, "Questions for Research and Development," in Wedel, Katz, and Weick, *Social Services by Government Contract*, pp. 86–87; Margaret Gibelman, "Title XX Purchase of Service: Some Speculations About Service Provision to the Poor," *Urban and Social Change Review* 13 (1980): 13; and Mildred Rein, "Fact and Function in Human Service Organizations," *Sociology and Social Research* 65 (1980): 87–90.
11. James C. Musselwhite, Jr., and Lester M. Salamon, *Social Welfare Policy and Privatization: Theory and Reality in Policymaking* (Washington, D.C.: The Urban Institute, 1986), p. 15; and David A. Grossman, Lester M. Salamon, and David M. Altschuler, *The New York Nonprofit Sector in a Time of Government Retrenchment* (Washington, D.C.: The Urban Institute, 1986), p. 57.
12. Yeheskel Hasenfeld, *Human Service Organizations* (Englewood Cliffs, N.J.: Prentice-Hall, 1983), pp. 9–11.
13. John Poertner and Charles A. Rapp, "Purchase of Service and Accountability: Will They Ever Meet?" *Administration in Social Work*, Spring 1985, pp. 57–66; George Thomas Haskett, "Contract Management and Monitoring in Public Social Service Agencies: A Study in Seven New York Agencies," D.S.W. dissertation, Columbia University, 1984; HSRI [Human Services Research Institute and Berkeley Planning Associates], *Assuring the Quality of Human Services: A Conceptual Analysis* (Washington, D.C.: Human Services Research Institute and Berkeley Planning Associates, 1980), pp. 137–38; Glenn Gritzer, *Interim Report—Regulation of Social Services* (New York: Community Service Society, 1980), pp. 3–4, 28; and Nelly Hartogs and Joseph Weber, *Impact of Government Funding on the Management of Voluntary Agencies* (New York: Greater New York Fund/United Way, 1978), p. 17.
14. See Robert T. Nakamura and Frank Smallwood, *The Politics of Policy*

Implementation (New York: St. Martin's, 1980); and Deil S. Wright, *Understanding Intergovernmental Relations/Public Policy and Participants' Perspectives in Local, State, and National Governments* (North Scituate, Mass.: Duxbury Press, 1978). Many nonprofit agency contracts are, in effect, subcontracts of intergovernmental contracts: "State and local governments administer about 60 percent of all government spending for social welfare programs. Half of this represents spending that originates with state and local government, and the other half spending that originates at the federal level but is administered by state and local authorities" (Musselwhite and Salamon, *Social Welfare Policy and Privatization*, p. 8).

15. See Bruce L. R. Smith, ed., *The New Political Economy: The Public Use of the Private Sector* (London: Macmillan, 1975); and Bruce L. R. Smith and D. C. Hague, *The Dilemma of Accountability in Modern Government: Independence vs. Control* (New York: St. Martin's, 1971). For a discussion of nonprofit agency autonomy and public accountability, see Kramer, *Voluntary Agencies*, pp. 288–92.

16. Operational problems also exist for contract administrators in the government funding organizations. See Peter M. Kettner and Lawrence L. Martin, *Purchase of Service Contracting* (Beverly Hills, Calif.: Sage Publications, 1987); Haskett, "Contract Management and Monitoring"; Ralph M. Kramer and Paul Terrell, *Social Services Contracting in the Bay Area* (Berkeley: Institute of Governmental Studies, University of California, Berkeley, 1984); and John D. Waller et al., *Monitoring for Government Agencies* (Washington, D.C.: The Urban Institute, 1976).

17. Daniel Jimenez, *A Study of Contracting Problems between Government Agencies and Non-Profit Organizations in California* (San Francisco: United Way of California, 1981), pp. 10–12; Hartogs and Weber, *Impact of Government Funding*, p. iv; and Robert Lefferts, *The Basic Handbook of Grants Management* (New York: Basic Books, 1983), pp. 79–80.

18. Hartogs and Weber, *Impact of Government Funding*, p. 53; Jimenez, *A Study of Contracting Problems*, p. 11; and Lefferts, *Basic Handbook*, pp. 84–85.

19. Jimenez, *A Study of Contracting Problems*, pp. 11–12.

20. See Jeremy Miransky, "Eleven Infallible Laws Governing the Negotiating Process Among Funding, Contractor and Client Agencies: By a Sadly Experienced Negotiator," *Journal of Sociology and Social Welfare*, June 1982, p. 305. The problematic nature of the contracting

process for the nonprofit agency administrator appears analogous to Lipsky's analysis of the individual in public services: "I locate the problem of street-level bureaucrats in the structure of their work" (Michael Lipsky, *Street-Level Bureaucracy* [New York: Russell Sage Foundation, 1980], p. xv).

21. Jimenez, *A Study of Contracting Problems*, pp. 15–18; Hartogs and Weber, *Impact of Government Funding*, pp. v, 24–25; and Dennis R. Young and Stephen J. Finch, *Foster Care and Nonprofit Agencies* (Lexington, Mass.: Lexington Books, 1977), pp. 234–38.

22. When the problems are unbearable for nonprofit agencies and their coalitions are powerful, however, these efforts emerge and system changes appear to be forced, as recently occurred in New York State. Agencies complained that they were having to get loans for payrolls because state agencies were taking months to execute and renew contracts. This problem prompted the governor and comptroller to establish a task force. Preliminary results included agreements by some state agencies to establish multiyear contracts and the creation of an interest-free loan fund available to nonprofits when formal contract approval is delayed. Marianne Arneberg et al., "Help for Community Groups," *Newsday*, May 15, 1989, p. 21.

23. Nelly Hartogs and Joseph Weber, *Managing Government Funded Programs in Voluntary Agencies* (New York: Greater New York Fund, 1979).

24. Lefferts, *Basic Handbook*, pp. 76–79.

25. Dennis R. Young, *Casebook of Management for Nonprofit Organizations—Entrepreneurship and Organizational Change in the Human Services.* (New York: The Haworth Press, 1985), pp. 19, 21.

26. Lefferts, *Basic Handbook*, pp. 85–92.

27. Kayla Conrad, "Promoting Quality of Care: The Role of the Compliance Director," *Child Welfare*, November–December, 1985, pp. 641, 647–48.

28. That managers would manipulate budgets and service statistics for the contract, client, or agency is consistent with research on organizational role orientations. See Robert Pruger, "On Resigning in Protest," *Administration in Social Work*, Winter 1979, pp. 453–63; W. Finch, "Administrative Priorities: The Impact of Employee Perception on Agency Functioning and Worker Satisfaction," *Administration in Social Work* (Winter 1977): pp. 391–400; Steven N. Brenner and Earl A. Molander, "Is the Ethics of Business Changing?" *Harvard Business Review*, January–February 1977, pp. 57–71; Irwin Epstein,

"Professional Role Orientations and Conflict Strategies," *Social Work*, October 1970, pp. 87–92; and Andrew Billingsley, "Bureaucratic and Professional Orientation Patterns in Social Casework," *Social Service Review*, December 1964, pp. 400–407.

29. Hartogs and Weber, *Impact of Government Funding*, p. 25.
30. Glenn Gritzer, *Interim Report—Regulation of Social Services* (New York: Community Service Society, 1980), pp. 22–23.
31. Ibid., pp. 17, 19–20; Karen Blumenthal, "Off Target? Job-Training Effort, Critics Say, Fails Many Who Need Help Most, *Wall Street Journal*, February 9, 1987, pp. 1, 15; and Nina Bernstein, "State Probes City Child Aid Agency," *Newsday*, April 13, 1988, p. 17.
32. The first significant empirical research on managers was reported by Carlson in 1951. See Henry Mintzberg, *The Nature of Managerial Work* (New York: Harper and Row, 1973), pp. 202–4. The emphasis in this discussion is on the evolution of the research question. The development of methodology in studying managerial behavior could also be examined as discrete approaches, each with its own evolution. For example, see Jane Hannaway, *Managers Managing: The Workings of an Administrative System* (New York: Oxford University Press, 1989), pp. 34–50.
33. The methods used to determine how managers spend their time were managers' diaries of daily activity, activity sampling, interviews and questionnaires, critical incident analysis, and structured and unstructured observation. Mintzberg, *The Nature of Managerial Work*, pp. 199–229.
34. Morgan W. McCall, Jr., Ann M. Morrison, and Robert L. Hannan, *Studies of Managerial Work: Results and Methods*, Technical Report Number 9 (Greensboro, N.C.: Center for Creative Leadership, 1978), p. 36.
35. Emerging from these studies of what managers do were six major research issues: whether managers control their work; whether effective and ineffective managers do things differently; what the content of managerial work is or whether it can be categorized; the relationship of organizational variables to the nature of managerial work; whether variability in managers' behavior can be explained by cycles in managerial work; and what the role of stress is in managers' patterns of work. Ibid., pp. 19–25.
36. To determine what roles managers assume, researchers use the same methods as those for determining how managers spend their time, but they apply factor analysis to the results.

37. Interpersonal roles are figurehead, leader, and liaison. Informational roles are monitor, disseminator, and spokesperson. Decisional roles are entrepreneur, disturbance handler, resource allocator, and negotiator (Mintzberg, *The Nature of Managerial Work*). Other studies have substantiated some of these findings. See Morgan W. McCall, Jr., and Cheryl A. Segrist, *In Pursuit of the Manager's Job: Building on Mintzberg*, Technical Report Number 14 (Greensboro, N.C.: Center for Creative Leadership, 1980); and Rino J. Patti, "Patterns of Management Activity in Social Welfare Agencies," in Simon Slavin, ed., *An Introduction to Human Services Management*, vol. 1 of *Social Administration: The Management of the Social Services*, 2d ed. (New York: The Haworth Press, 1985), pp. 28–43.

38. Leonard R. Sayles, *Managerial Behavior: Administration in Complex Organizations* (New York: McGraw-Hill, 1964), p. viii, as quoted in Mintzberg, *The Nature of Managerial Work*, p. 218; and Leonard R. Sayles, *Leadership: What Effective Managers Really Do . . . and How They Do It* (New York: McGraw-Hill, 1979), p. 210.

39. Morgan W. McCall, Jr., and Robert E. Kaplan, *Whatever It Takes: Decision Makers at Work* (Englewood Cliffs, N.J.: Prentice-Hall, 1985), pp. xi–xii. The framework McCall and Kaplan use to report their findings can be translated into the following questions: How does a problem become defined as such by the manager? What determines whether the manager acts on the problem? How does the manager decide what to do? After doing something about the problem, how does the manager cope with the outcome? The answers to these questions, which in practice are not necessarily asked or dealt with sequentially, are discussed by McCall and Kaplan in concrete, behavioral terms. For example, they offer "some words of advice" to managers for setting priorities among problems. Their advice is categorized as follows: Do it now, do it later, do it earlier, do two things at once, do it anyway, do it your way (pp. 50–55).

40. Since managers "employ maps of their world to help them see what is relevant to their work," McCall and Kaplan discuss the importance of identifying managers' cognitive maps (ibid., p. 24). This is also a key construct in ethnomethodology. See David M. Fetterman, *Ethnography: Step by Step*, Applied Social Research Methods Series, vol. 17 (Newbury Park, Calif.: Sage Publications, 1989), p. 16; Matthew B. Miles and A. Michael Huberman, *Qualitative Data Analysis: A Sourcebook of New Methods* (Beverly Hills, Calif.: Sage Publications, 1984), p. 249; and James P. Spradley, *The Ethnographic Interview* (New

York: Holt, Rinehart and Winston, 1979), p. 7. For a comprehensive discussion of the original concept of cognitive maps, see Ulrich Neisser, *Cognition and Reality: Principles and Implications of Cognitive Psychology* (New York: Freeman, 1976), pp. 108–27.

41. Gareth Morgan, *Images of Organization* (Newbury Park, Calif.: Sage Publications, 1986), pp. 339–40. Morgan (pp. 345–46) summarizes the extensive literature on "the impact of metaphor on the way we think, on our language, and on systems of scientific and everyday knowledge." He discusses the strengths and limitations of eight metaphors of organization: as machines, organisms, brains, cultures, political systems, psychic prisons, flux and transformation, and instruments of domination.

42. Gareth Morgan, *Creative Organization Theory: A Resourcebook* (Newbury Park, Calif.: Sage Publications, 1989), p. 8.

43. Rosabeth Moss Kanter, *When Giants Learn to Dance: Mastering the Challenges of Strategy, Management, and Careers in the 1990s* (New York: Simon and Schuster, 1989), pp. 9–12; Rosabeth Moss Kanter, *The Change Masters: Innovation and Entrepreneurship in the American Corporation* (New York: Simon and Schuster, 1983), pp. 371–85; Rosabeth Moss Kanter, *Men and Women of the Corporation* (New York: Basic Books, 1977), pp. 291–98; Barbara Ley Toffler, *Tough Choices: Managers Talk Ethics* (New York: John Wiley and Sons, 1986), p. 3; and Dennis R. Young, *Casebook of Management for Nonprofit Organizations—Entrepreneurship and Organizational Change in the Human Services* (New York: The Haworth Press, 1985), pp. 3–4. Although Kanter (*Men and Women of the Corporation,* p. vi) is the only one identifying her research as such, all three have used ethnographic methods.

44. For data on the scope of contracting in New York State and the United States, see Avner Ben-Ner and Theresa Van Hoomissen, *A Study of the Nonprofit Sector in New York State: Its Size, Nature, and Economic Impact* (Albany, N.Y.: Nelson A. Rockefeller Institute of Government, State University of New York, 1989), pp. 91–114; Sharon S. Dawes and Judith R. Saidel, *The State and the Voluntary Sector: A Report of New York State Project 2000* (Albany, N.Y.: Nelson A. Rockefeller Institute of Government, State University of New York, 1988), p. 19; Musselwhite and Salamon, *Social Welfare Policy and Privatization,* p. 9; and Kramer and Terrell, *Social Services Contracting,* pp. 40–41. For a discussion of the lack of relevant research, see Harold W. Demone, Jr., and Margaret Gibelman, "In Search of a

Theoretical Base for the Purchase of Services," in Harold W. Demone, Jr., and Margaret Gibelman, eds., *Services for Sale: Purchasing Health and Human Services* (New Brunswick, N.J.: Rutgers University Press, 1989), pp. 5–6.

45. His focus is different, but for another attempt to portray managers' work lives, see Young, *Casebook of Management*.

46. Transcripts of the interviews were analyzed with the assistance of a computer software program, The Ethnograph Version 3.0, Qualis Research Associates, Littleton, Colorado. For a comprehensive discussion of methodology, the interview procedure, and use of The Ethnograph, see Susan R. Bernstein, "Playing the Game of Contracted Services: Administrative, Ethical, and Political Issues for the Nonprofit Agency Manager," D.S.W. dissertation, City University of New York, 1989, pp. 45–95, 504–11. For discussions of the importance of replicability and documentation, see Jerome Kirk and Marc L. Miller, *Reliability and Validity in Qualitative Research*, Qualitative Research Methods, vol. 1 (Beverly Hills, Calif.: Sage Publications, 1986), p. 72; and Miles and Huberman, *Qualitative Data Analysis*, pp. 243–44.

47. Fetterman, *Ethnography*, p. 21; and Barney G. Glaser and Anselm L. Strauss, *The Discovery of Grounded Theory: Strategies for Qualitative Research* (New York: Aldine de Gruyter, 1967), p. 249.

48. GFO funding is sometimes dependent on accreditation by the Joint Commission, and its standards are often appropriated by GFOs.

49. For example, Kettner and Martin, *Purchase of Service Contracting*, make a distinction, based on "ownership of client, services, and financial information," between procurement (contracts) and assistance (grants). Others distinguish between purchase of service and block contracting. The distinction is that in purchase of service the GFO buys units of service (typically, by client or groups of clients) only as necessary, and in block contracting the GFO commits to buy a certain number of units in advance. See Arnold Gurin and Barry Friedman, *Contracting for Service as a Mechanism for the Delivery of Human Services: A Study of Contracting Practices in Three Human Service Agencies in Massachusetts*, the Florence Heller Graduate School for Advanced Studies in Social Welfare, Brandeis University for the Office of Human Development Services (Washington, D.C.: National Technical Information Service, U.S. Department of Commerce, 1980).

THE GAME OF
CONTRACTED SERVICES

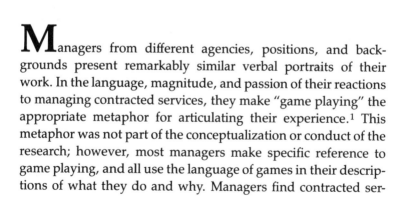

Managers from different agencies, positions, and backgrounds present remarkably similar verbal portraits of their work. In the language, magnitude, and passion of their reactions to managing contracted services, they make "game playing" the appropriate metaphor for articulating their experience.[1] This metaphor was not part of the conceptualization or conduct of the research; however, most managers make specific reference to game playing, and all use the language of games in their descriptions of what they do and why. Managers find contracted services "crazy"; the game metaphor keeps them from succumbing to "craziness."

The paradoxical nature of contracted services makes the metaphor compelling. Managers talk of being very serious about what they do, but of not taking contract compliance too seriously. Many are managers in NPAs in which over 90 percent of the funding is from GFOs, yet the NPA mission is the most crucial factor in their decision making. Repeatedly, managers describe situations in which aspects of the management of contracted services conflict with reality. In accepting these paradoxes, managers perceive their task as a game. This perception enables them to understand, get control of, and keep in perspective contracted services.

One manager, in describing the qualities her NPA should seek if she had to be replaced, uses the game metaphor to stress the importance of understanding the GFO system.

> I think you have to be the kind of person who's interested in how the system works. If you can understand how all the pieces fit together, it's not quite so onerous. I've always approached it from the point that if you can understand why you have to fill out the form and what it generates and how it fits into the whole larger system, filling out the form doesn't become quite so bad. It has a meaning. It's not just an exercise in filling out a form. You have to have that interest because we're a small program, but we fit in somewhere. When we object to certain things, and [GFO] say, "But if we have this piece of information, then that can happen," then giving them that piece of information isn't quite so tough. I think that, to me, that's the game of it.

Another manager describes the system as "overwhelming" but also "fun" and explains, "If you start to take it so, so seriously, you would just be really nuts." She describes her feelings about her job in language that could be used to explain the exhilaration that comes from getting control of any difficult game of skill.

It's always a new dilemma every day. Just to figure out how to send those UCRs [uniform case records] down [to the GFO] without [the GFO's] losing them—that's a problem that's fun to solve.

There's something about being a part of the [GFO] system that's a challenge. To know that it doesn't make sense for [the GFO] not to fund a [particular program]. It just doesn't make sense. So that, in a way, I know that I'm writing something that they have to fund. It's fun to start figuring out how it works.

It gives you a sense of real mastery when you've learned how and where and what system to address one's needs to. A real sense of mastery. It's like when you drive a stick-shift car—I found that fun, while it was scary as anything in the beginning. So, now it's fun because we have a track record of having gotten funded two proposals—learning the numbers, being able to give the jargon back, to be able to communicate in their language, with their figures, but not take it so, so seriously at this end.[2]

For another manager, the game metaphor is a way of keeping the paradoxical, crazy quality of managing contracted services in perspective.

I guess it's always been part of my personality and the way that I am that you can only take these things just so seriously. It's like—when you fill out the UCRs—there are some people who are really very, very serious about this, and you have to do it all precisely and you have to include absolutely everything in this and it has to be correct and you have to use this as a tool. My feeling is you fill it out as best as you can, you hit the points that you have to, but don't put all of your time and your effort into a form. Put your time and your effort into a client and into service delivery.

So that's what I mean when I say it's a game. Not that I'm saying don't take it seriously and don't do it as best as you can, but don't obsess about it, because you'll get crazy.

Playing the Game

A manager who has directed a foundation-funded NPA program for many years explains why she seeks a GFO contract and what it is like when she gets it.

> We were always having to put so much energy into looking for funding that the reality was that the service piece always suffered for about three months a year. Then it suffered because we were always anxious whether we'd have jobs. Then, everyone [foundation funders] kept telling us, "Get into the system. Get into the system. Get into the system." We finally just said, "Okay."
> We were all new, green at this whole system. The first week we had gone to [GFO] training, and they started rattling off these numbers and we thought, "Oh God, we're intelligent people. How are we ever going to figure this out?" It seemed so overwhelming. So we [NPA managers] started this group, to commiserate and support each other and to learn from each other in the beginning days because no one knew how these programs were going to fit in with [NPA] systems.

Coping with conflicts with reality is a consuming task for managers.

> We're very active. We always comment to the city on everything. We're notorious for sending them letters about everything, going to meetings, complaining, and giving them unsolicited advice.

Reality—the truth, the fact, the way things are—is, of course, as managers perceive it. That their perception is correct is often verified by the GFO's yielding "to reality."

Contract requirements may conflict with the purpose of the service. A manager's frustration with a youth services contract is that the way it is written and monitored does not "take into consideration you're dealing with kids."

> So you [the GFO] come and you don't see a hundred on the playground. I mean be real. Be real. That's on a piece of paper. We're talking about kids. These are human beings and there are a hundred other things they could be involved in—so understand that.

While some monitors do "understand that," others "are very sticky" about "holding" NPAs to whatever the contract says.

Another manager expresses her fury with a GFO requirement, eventually abandoned, that a contracted dropout prevention program be restricted to the academic year.

> They [GFO] said you're funded for ten months. I said, "What are we supposed to do with the staff?" They said, "Let them go and rehire." I said, "Oh—and that's why you have dropouts." That was a battle.

The manager of a different dropout prevention program explains what he does when the GFO does not fund the "whole list of things that we had to do" contractually and the NPA is incapable of providing them without funding. In a program for seventh graders, the GFO includes career/vocational counseling in the list of required services.

> How much of that are we going to do? In reality, we're not going to do that. We're going to help the kids fill out Summer Youth Employment job applications, and maybe

we'll help the kids get some jobs, but as a whole, we're not in a position to do that.

An executive director describes the "incredible" loan contract the GFO expects her NPA to sign for the renovation of a residence for the homeless. The contract conflicts with the purpose of the service in its stipulation that for twenty years neither the building use be changed nor the loan prepaid.

> Our attorneys and our board of directors took issue with that and it took us a long time to come to the point of negotiating with them [GFO] that after ten years, we could pay the remainder of the loan and have the only restriction on the building be that it would provide housing and supportive services to the homeless or people of low income.

Contract requirements often conflict with the capability of GFOs to uphold their contractual obligations. For example, the seemingly simple task of delivering mandated reports on children in foster care to the correct GFO unit can require herculean effort because the GFO does not have accurate records on which units have which cases.

> We've got a UCR that came back telling us that the unit that it's been in has been dissolved six months. They [GFO] cannot find the [child's] case record. They do not know what unit is now covering the case.

The burden is now on this manager to track down the correct GFO unit. This involves making multiple calls to various GFO offices and, eventually, to the computer-systems people.

> "Look, this is our problem—we can't locate where this case is, if it's anywhere. Can you find out anything?" They'll call back and say, "Well, the case record's been

lost," or "Yeah, the worker is over on such and such, but they haven't done anything with the case and, therefore, nothing has come up under their number."

The manager explains the GFO worker may not have "done anything" because there is no indication that there is an immediate problem and the case record is in a "stack of 170."

Another manager explains the absurdity of a new level of service standard established by the GFO for homemaker services.

> One of their [GFO's] initial plans was that they would require each of our case coordinators to be responsible for thirty-five families receiving homemaker services, on the premise that each family had a [GFO] social worker. It's true they have, on paper, [GFO] workers, and in the best of all possible worlds, if [the GFO] were able to function better, the [GFO] worker could realistically take care of the family's needs. But in the real world, [the GFO] can't take care of these cases and can't address the crises as quickly as they need to be addressed.

Asked how she accounts for the GFO's eventually reducing the required level of service, which her NPA "argued in a big way about," she replies, "Reality must have impinged on them."

The contracting process itself often conflicts with reality. Given that her NPA's contracts are consistently renewed, a manager bemoans the absurdity of the annual cycle.

> In my mind, there should be—you meet program objectives, the funding stream is there, it's a very simple renewal process, and you renegotiate your budget. To do this every year, the cost of this, for them and for us—it's crazy. But, no one's talking about it.

Another manager describes the "real catch-22" of making a case for additional funding when contract requirements virtually guarantee that all current funds are not spent. Underutilization of services, leading to accruals, is a result of staffing realities.

> For instance, I have a worker closing a case who's going on a month's vacation starting Monday. Now, he's going to take my utilization down, but I'm not going to assign a new case to him now when he's going to be gone for a whole month. They [GFO] don't want to hear from that. Workers who are brand new—they expect you're going to hand them twelve cases as they walk through the door, and I won't do that.
>
> If you have had a worker with an extended illness and maybe you have fallen in the number of contacts, we may still be covering the case because the case aide is in there, but they only count the case planner's contacts.

One manager expresses her exasperation at the impossibility of the NPA's planning for additional services because of the GFO's approach to planning.

> I said to the guy at the city, "Why are you contracting with somebody else? Why don't you give us a chance to expand?" He said, "Well, we gave you the chance to expand. We would call you up and offer you a case." I said, "Yeah, but calling me up and saying, 'Can you take a case tomorrow or can you take two cases the next day?'—that's not a plan to expand. We need something like, 'Your program size is going to be twenty-five or fifty or seventy-five or one hundred cases bigger.' We'll hire the workers and the homemakers, and we'll pick up the cases. We can't just accrete them a day here or a day there."

To varying degrees, NPAs depend on timely, equitable payment from GFOs to provide the contracted service. GFO rules and procedures for payment often conflict with the reality of an NPA's dependence on this payment. A "major irritant" for one manager is the reimbursement contract.

> I have to have the private money available to pay for things, and then I get reimbursed, which puts me in this crazy position of having all this money budgeted, but if I don't have the cash to spend it, then I can't get the money back. So I may have four thousand dollars in supplies. If I don't have any cash on hand, I can't go out and buy supplies.

GFO reimbursement is typically two months after his NPA has submitted receipts. Since salary is the priority, any other expenditures are delayed.

> And what happened last year was, finally at the end, they gave us money, the last two weeks of the year. We spent something like forty thousand dollars in two weeks' time so that we could get it spent by June 30, which is obviously not the best way.

One manager decries the complexity of GFO hurdles that need to be overcome to obtain authorization for payment for renovations to contracted service offices, despite the reality that the program has existed for over a decade and will, in all likelihood, continue.

> They [GFO] are so concerned about anybody they contract with ripping them off—it's like fighting your way through a thorn hedge or something to get through all the rules and regulations.

This fight, involving her NPA's attorney, is a "major headache," which is "highly nerve-wracking."

After getting a GFO to agree that the purchase date for a $279 item is acceptable, another manager's exasperation, when the expenditure is rejected for being over $100, is palpable. He talks to his monitor, who is authorized to issue waivers.

> "You know I'm not taking the $279 and putting it in my pocket. I'm not just buying balloons with it. I bought an SRA [educational] kit. The kids use it. It's useful. It's going to have a long lifetime, and you know I'm getting a contract next year. It's not going to be abused."
> I was furious by this time. I was practically in tears. She said, "Can't you pay for this out of some other category?" I said, "I don't have the money. I don't have any other money." She could tell [I was at the end of my rope]. She said, "Well, this time I'll approve it, but don't let this happen again."

Even when the GFO has authorized payment, the process of getting a check is an enormous problem for some managers. A GFO's computerized system to keep track of which foster children are in whose care is used to determine GFO funds owed NPAs. However, according to the compliance coordinator in a large agency, this system is "so inaccurate" that it is "a tremendous pain" to prepare her NPA's monthly bill to the GFO.

> For every single difference [in whom the GFO says we are serving and whom we are actually serving], we have to make out a form. It's absolutely horrendous. The whole billing system now is very time consuming and very frustrating.

The executive director of a small agency feels that GFOs do not grasp the significance of timely payment. Asked to hold a check so the director can pick it up, the GFO agrees, but then mails it. When the check is lost in the mail, the GFO will not reissue it for three weeks. The implications are serious.

Right now, I haven't collected my paycheck for this month. Luckily, my tax return came. We borrowed money from [a loan fund]. You scramble the best you can. What we're going to do in the long term is the board has committed themselves to coming up with a cash reserve fund of $50,000 or more to try to help with this problem. We try to get foundations—you know somebody's going to pay you a grant, maybe you can get them to give it to you a month early. You scramble. You hold off on paying anything you don't have to pay. And have a lot of anxiety attacks, let me assure you.

Given the conflicts with reality in the other dimensions of contracting, it follows that conflicts exist in the evaluation process as well. An executive director expresses her skepticism about the validity of the GFO's primary criteria for assessing preventive services.

The first two years, our program was a success. I get very dubious about these statistics—it was a success because none of the children in the families we worked with were removed from the home. This past year, in two families, the children had to be removed.

She attributes the lack of "success" to the increase in drugs and to overcrowded housing, factors that the GFO does not consider in its evaluation of outcome.

The same executive director points out that unrealistic criteria for the accomplishment of interim objectives also conflict with clients' reality. The GFO neither recognizes nor reimburses advocacy. For example, every month for four years, her NPA advocates for housing for a particular family but the first time this effort counts is the month the family moves.

Another manager expresses a conviction that a GFO's evaluation system has no relationship to the reality of client needs, the program delivered, or fiduciary responsibility.

The [GFO] has such a mindset, they're so schizoid about accountability. On the one hand, the system is totally devoid of accountability. Devoid. On the other hand, they think they've got all these structures that provide accountability, and they thought this was a way to assure accountability.

It doesn't assure accountability. Yes, somebody can give the [GFO director] a memo saying the programs are doing X, Y, and Z, but it doesn't mean that they are. And ultimately it doesn't mean that the kids are getting what they need.

After summarizing the problems resulting from performance-based contracting, a manager explains, in the most poignant way, why she feels the demands of playing the game conflict with the ability to affect these problems.

Why I don't think it's being dealt with is because I think you've got social workers—and I use myself as an example—who are drowning, who are trying to go after every penny we can find in terms of services for people, trying to get workers to work to greater productivity, and we're running in place and we're using all our energy spinning our wheels. Because government contracts are where the money is. If that's what the government's demanding, that's what we do. If they want us to stand on our heads, we stand on our heads. I almost believe we don't have the energy, and maybe we don't feel we have the power.

Dynamics

What are the forces motivating or inducing managers to act, or not act, as they do?[3] What keeps them so involved despite all the craziness? Enjoyment has been conceptualized as "the holistic sensation that people feel when they act with total involvement—as flow."[4] A description of the experience of flow when playing chess is strikingly similar to what administrators say about managing contracted services.

> Flow in chess, as in other activities, depends on a very delicate balance between being in control and being overwhelmed. It is this tension that forces the player to attend to the game, with the resulting high pitch of concentration and involvement.[5]

The drive to accomplish a goal emerges repeatedly. The goal can be an overriding sense of mission and purpose about the work or an intermediate objective toward achievement of that goal. Goals are often multiple; typically, they conflict. Analyzing the way managers choose to act is crucial in understanding the significance of this drive: "Effective managers have a vision for the business that makes sense of unrelated problems and actions."[6]

In describing the relationship of NPAs to GFOs as cordially adversarial, a manager stresses her NPA's mission and the perception of that mission by GFOs.

> I think, as an agency, people know that we are extremely serious about what we do, that we are determined to do it well, and we are also determined to do it as much as we can in conformance to the way in which we want to deliver [services], so that we will argue, and we will go to the mat, and we will mobilize, and whatever.

Many managers find navigation of the playing field extraordinarily complex. An executive director says, "It's a puzzle; if you like puzzles then you're okay." In the beginning, she says she was "really in the dark" about the contracting process for special legislative grants.

You go through so many different senseless steps, and I think once you go through it the first time and they know who you are and things have gone through without any incident, then things come fairly quickly—even though we have not yet received [the monies for the first contract year], and I have right here and am just finishing, the application for the second round.

Managers who have worked in GFOs feel that experience makes it easier to navigate the GFOs. One manager who does not have GFO experience but thinks it would have been valuable, explains, "It is a help to know how their mind, how the bureaucratic mind, works."

Surviving the competition is complex in the management of contracted services. An NPA's competitors can be GFOs, other NPAs, or, increasingly, for-profit organizations. While managers express great fervor about their battles with GFOs, their objective is most often to endure in what they understand to be an ongoing, unending struggle. Competition with other NPAs is usually just alluded to by managers. A great deal of cooperative effort among NPAs is directed toward GFOs; however, they are competing for the same GFO resources.

An executive director explains that while a GFO funds some NPAs in full for programs, his and others are required to match a portion of the contract amount. However, he says, "The reality of it is basically that you try to hold on to what you've got." As the result of a demographic evaluation of need, the GFO cuts funding for programs in his community, and his NPA is "slashed" $40,000. He is concerned that the remaining funding is in jeopardy because the GFO's director has changed since the last contracts were issued: "I don't know what's going to happen. I just hold my breath."

The GFO can be formidable competition. An executive director describes what happens when NPAs try to change the planned implementation of a home-care program for the elderly.

> The city [GFO] kept saying in the meetings they did have: "This is the way it is." And the whole city [NPAs] was up in arms over this. No matter how much we talked, it didn't work. The city [GFO] just went ahead like a juggernaut.

When a manager hears the GFO is going to contract with additional NPAs for homemaking services, she suspects an issue of competition.

> I may be imagining this, but my suspicion is they [GFO] are going to contract with vendors at a lower rate, and the only way anybody can do this at a lower rate is to sacrifice the quality. We have two MSWs and two BAs, and we try to offer the homemakers a decent wage, as decent as we can make it, and try to treat the homemakers fairly and do a good job on the training and provide the support. Some of that's going to have to go with a lower rate.

Mastering the rules is extraordinarily complex; this is not a game with one rule book. Rules are clear and unclear, explicit and implicit, enforced and not enforced. They are ever changing. What is acceptable one year may not be the next. What is acceptable to one monitor may not be to another.

To be able to affect the terms of his contract, an executive director describes the necessity of learning "how things work" in the state legislature.

> There's a legislative committee of [the NPA coalition]. You stay on top of bills that are being introduced and so forth and you just see how the game is played because you're there. So when we develop strategy then that's part of the information that flows into our leadership: This is what they want to see, this is how it should be presented.

Another manager explains what happens when the GFO changes a rule without informing NPAs and then penalizes them for violating it.

It caused a bit of a disturbance because [NPA coalition] also does a lot of the contract negotiations for the agencies, and their people hadn't spotted it either. Nobody was really aware of it. So all of a sudden you had a whole group of agencies that were quite upset that someone had pulled the wool over their eyes and slipped something through.

They [GFO and NPA coalition] came to terms verbally on how if something was changed, how it would be indicated. But they never made a commitment in writing that all changes must be in bold, with the old in italics and the replacement in bold. Nothing like that, anything that's formal. They came to a verbal agreement, basically, that changes should be identifiable. Nobody wanted to be pinned down.

For managers, strategies for dealing with GFOs are a necessity. Most express the need for having a philosophical perspective on affecting GFOs. One manager explains, in describing her efforts to get changes in a contract:

Going in [to the GFO] you can't really expect very much of a response. And, whatever response you want, you have to create.

In a similar vein, another manager says:

I don't think they [GFO] like or dislike me per se, but there's a mutual respect. I may not agree with the priorities that are selected down at their end because I would have different priorities, but then I realize that I need to work with them. It's something I cannot control, but I will attempt to influence them.

Many managers talk of the need for positioning the NPA to affect the GFO.

Actually our program assessment statistics have improved on a yearly basis, and I just think it's a game. I think it's a question on a lot of levels of what kind of systems can you put in place.

All managers believe an NPA coalition strategy is essential. According to one manager:

It keeps you tuned into what's happening, and it also means you don't have to fight your battles alone all the time. When city contract time comes around and there're all these issues about how the contract is written, we worry all the time. We don't all have to go singly and try to tackle [the GFO], and we all have our say. And, [NPA coalition] has more and more meetings, just because issues have become so much more complicated.

The challenge of managing contracted services is constant for some managers. For one, who feels she has mastered management of her program, the challenge is being involved in contracting issues affecting all NPAs funded by her GFO. She explains how and why she makes the time to be involved in this way.

I really like this. I get very fed up with the routine; I've done this for a long time. It's getting pretty boring, but I've been lucky being on these [NPA coalition] committees, and I really have found that's a whole new challenge and new learning in terms of trying to work out procedures. There're a few of us who've been tapped by [NPA coalition] as being people who are willing to make the time, and I am. I'd rather go out and do that and sit at night and read progress notes than sitting here in the office all day. I seem to so far be able to manage both.

After a successful NPA coalition fight with a GFO, her attitude and that of many of her colleagues changed.

All of these things have made us very aware and much more willing to not just sit and do what's handed to you, but be an active participant. Obviously, it has some limitations, but I really find it a learning experience. Somehow, that great big, thick, boilerplate contract doesn't look quite so long.

Despite all the craziness and complexity, many managers express enjoyment when they describe their work. Research indicates this feeling of pleasure, under trying circumstances, is not at all contradictory: "Apparently, something that is enjoyable to do gives a feeling of creative discovery, a challenge overcome, a difficulty resolved."[7] One manager, who feels that doing her job is "an art," explains how she deals with GFOs.

I'm conniving if I want something, like if I go into contract negotiations. I have told the city [GFO] on a number of occasions: "We won't take the contract unless you give us what we want." And sometimes it works and sometimes not. We walk out. It's just like seductiveness. It's a chess game, and I can do that. So we do a little acting-out behavior, but that's what I like about it. That's fun.

NOTES

1. While social work administration has apparently never been conceptualized as a game, politics, business, and even living itself, particularly in the United States, have. See Hedrick Smith, *The Power Game: How Washington Works* (New York: Random House, 1988), for a recent book using the game metaphor for politics. For applications of the game metaphor in business, see Ardis Burst and Leonard A. Schlesinger, *The Management Game* (New York: Viking, 1987); Betty Lehan Harragan, *Games Mother Never Taught You: Corporate Gamesmanship for Women* (New York: Warner Books, 1977); Rosabeth Moss Kanter, *When Giants Learn to Dance: Mastering the Challenges of Strategy,*

Management, and Careers in the 1990s (New York: Simon and Schuster, 1989), pp. 18–22; Robert Keidel, *Game Plans: Sports Strategies for Business* (New York: E. P. Dutton, 1985); Robert Keidel, *Game Plans: Designs for Working and Winning Together* (New York: John Wiley and Sons, 1988); and Michael Maccoby, *The Gamesman: The New Corporate Leaders* (New York: Simon and Schuster, 1976). "All life is a game of power" is the thesis of Michael Korda, *Power! How to Get It, How to Use It* (New York: Random House, 1975), p. 3. For a comprehensive application of the game concept to organizations, see Michael Crozier and Erhard Friedberg, *Actors and Systems: The Politics of Collective Action* (Chicago: University of Chicago Press, 1980), pp. 45–63.

2. The "mastery" and sense of control the manager feels in playing the game of contracted services parallels Smith's analysis of politics in *The Power Game*: "Some like to say that the power game is an unpredictable casino of chance and improvisation. But most of the time politics is about as casual and offhand as the well-practiced triple flips of an Olympic high diver" (p. xvii).

3. The benefits of answering this question are analogous to those of conceptualizing politics as a game: "Sometimes it explains why some good people don't play the game better, why they don't win." Ibid., p. xvii.

4. Mihaly Csikszentmihalyi, *Beyond Boredom and Anxiety: The Experience of Play in Work and Games* (San Francisco: Jossey-Bass, 1975), p. 36. See also Mihaly Csikszentmihalyi, *Flow: The Psychology of Optimal Experience* (New York: Harper and Row, 1990); and Mihaly Csikszentmihalyi and Isabella S. Csikszentmihalyi, eds., *Optimal Experience: Psychological Studies of Flow in Consciousness* (Cambridge: Cambridge University Press, 1988).

5. Csikszentmihalyi, *Beyond Boredom and Anxiety*, p. 64.

6. Morgan W. McCall, Jr., and Robert E. Kaplan, *Whatever It Takes: Decision Makers at Work* (Englewood Cliffs, N.J.: Prentice-Hall, 1985), p. 82.

7. Csikszentmihalyi, *Beyond Boredom and Anxiety*, p. 181.

PERSPECTIVES

Whatever drives managers to play the game of contracted services, they do so with a striking clarity of purpose. NPA managers have unique perspectives based on education and experience. These perspectives help them sort out the administrative, ethical, and political issues they confront and help them frame their strategies for dealing with GFOs.[1]

Several managers, for different reasons, characterize NPAs and GFOs as partners. Because one executive director's NPA, which serves the homeless, believes government and NPAs should be "working in a partnership," the director seeks government funding, even though the pursuit requires more time and effort than does private fund raising. Her NPA does not want the GFO "to respond so much that we can sit back and just walk away and go and find a new business to be about," but it does want the GFO to "meet us halfway," by providing the policy, financial, and material support so the NPA is "able to run those programs."

Another manager, new to the New York City child welfare system, is shocked by the "bad blood" between the GFO and NPAs, manifest in the GFO's view that "the private agencies only want to work with the easy cases, that we will skim off the cream and leave them the others." She says, "I don't believe, fundamentally, that those of us who are supposed to be of service to the wider community, and especially to poor families, should be competing with each other or denigrating each other's efforts."

A compliance coordinator believes that a partnership between NPAs and the city GFO, "working as a 'we' team," is essential.

> We realized that if we did not work together there was absolutely no way either of us, as agencies or the city, were going to survive the system. Either the system would go or we'd go. The system was mandated by state law. So we were in a bad position. We also had a common target because the state was saying, "You will do this," and they were not listening to anybody. So we kind of did the reverse of divide and conquer: We combined to fight the common enemy.

Another manager conceptualizes her NPA's relationships with GFOs as "cordially adversarial," because her NPA is serious about delivering services in its own way, despite GFO constraints. She describes her strategy for relating to GFOs.

> We recognize whenever we can that we are in the same business and that though we come in with some different

perspectives, with different priorities, they're not necessarily the bad guys, and we're the good guys. Hopefully it's a constructive working relationship that is honest. The differences are on the table. If I'm going to go over somebody's head or I'm going to the mat on something or I'm going to potentially embarrass somebody, I will tell people.

Many managers refer to GFOs as a disorganized "mess." This disorganization exists in part by definition, because the GFO is typically many autonomous organizations, with different levels of government and different departments of government within each level. The sense of chaos is so overpowering for some managers that their objective is simply to avoid being engulfed by it. One manager describes her strategy for getting mandatory reports to "the edge of the void."

We refuse to send the original, even though in theory it's supposed to be sent. Nobody I know sends original UCRs [uniform case records]. We've never, rarely—because we're afraid it'll get lost in the black void.

Another manager, saying it can take many months for the GFO to consider budget modifications, pictures documents sent to them as going "down the rabbit hole."

Some managers find the GFO chaos baffling. Although a program director once worked for the GFO that now funds her NPA, she says, "I still don't know why" they cannot issue contracts when a program starts, instead of eight months later. An executive director, trying to explain why a contract for services administered through one state GFO the previous year is to be granted through a different GFO this year, says, "I think it's probably ad hoc; it makes no sense, so I can't imagine how they decide." Another manager says, given "convoluted" GFO procedures,

"No wonder they have such chaos, no wonder their workers don't know how to do what they're supposed to do." She likes and respects the GFO person who writes many of the procedures, and so she marvels, "I don't know where it goes wrong. It's just cumbersome."

For other managers, chaos results from the intractability of the social problems GFOs confront. An executive director thinks the child welfare system "is out of control" and legislation has not caught up to the problem. Another manager, a veteran caseworker, qualifies her criticism of chaotic GFO services because, "These cases are tough; nobody knows what to do with these families."

Several managers perceive as the cause of the chaos the city GFOs' lack of control over program structure because of their acquiescence to the mandates of state GFOs. An executive director decries the city's unwillingness, despite its obvious leverage, to fight state regulations on the structure of a new home-care program for the elderly.

New York City is different from the state—you can't take a statewide program and impose it on the city. The [city GFO] as the largest [agency for the aging] should have taken the advocacy role. They abdicated it. So what they've basically become is just a pass-through, where they take state regulations and they take state money. Their whole thing was, "Well, if we didn't move on it quickly, we would have lost the money."

That's ridiculous, though, because the state is not going to risk losing the largest contractor, the city [GFO]. They're not going to. If the [city GFO] said, "Look, we have to promulgate our own rules and regulations; we need six months to do it," the state is not going to say, "Tough nuggies. You lost the money." They'll fight against it but in the end will say, "Sure, if that's what it has to be—we're not happy about it, but go ahead."

Some managers attribute the chaos to GFOs' lack of control over their staffing. One manager deplores a GFO's inability to maintain quality staff, a result of their not hiring, respecting, paying, or supervising staff "in a way that's professional." For another manager, the chaos emerges from rapid turnover among senior GFO staff, with the concomitant changes in directives. These changes have "burned" him and his colleagues, and they determine, "You can't just depend upon somebody's word." A compliance coordinator believes the chaos follows from the GFO's inability to have the staff work efficiently because of written and unwritten union rules.

All managers believe that the autonomy of different levels of government and of different departments on the same level results in a stupefying lack of coordination. A compliance coordinator describes what "the overlap between levels of government" means for his NPA.

> All of them choose to write their requirements in slightly different ways. All of them have separate processes for monitoring and evaluating. There's a sense both of overload and of how many different masters can we have.
>
> So that, to choose the most extreme case, we have some systems where they'll change their requirements every year or two. Joint Commission has a new manual every two years. And state regulations are always changing and city requirements are often changing. So that we can get in a situation where it becomes a forest. We tell our case-workers: "Here is the new case recording format. You must learn it because we have to deal with all these reporting requirements." And six months later, we tell our case-workers: "Here are the new recording requirements." And, six months after that. Terrible waste for the worker.

For other managers, the most frustrating manifestation of the lack of coordination is within the same governmental level. One relates the absurd situation when he, not the GFO (a school district), informs a principal that there is going to be a joint NPA/GFO program in his school with his staff. Another executive director is "angry" because the GFO staff responsible for planning "have never picked the brains" of their own on-site monitors, who know the most about the contracted programs.

The lack of coordination is severe when offices within a GFO are antagonistic. An executive director explains that a GFO contracting office, to avoid having the same GFO's legal office "looking over their shoulder," ignores her request for contractual changes. A manager describes a different GFO as being "fragmented in everything they do," resulting in NPAs' "constantly, constantly being bounced around."

NPA managers, struggling for scarce resources themselves, bristle at obvious inefficiency and waste in GFO operations. Noting the "astronomical" turnover in GFO protective services workers, an executive director says she has "a lot of compassion" for the workers because of the "planned dysfunction" of their work environment: three hundred staff working in "such a maze, in an ocean of paper" in "a huge, open office with desks piled with files, the phones going, and cardboard boxes all around." There is not much improvement even when the GFO moves two thirds of these staff to "a very nice building."

> They set it up with a telephone system with no intercoms on the phones. Every worker has his or her own number. If they're not sitting in their cubby and the phone rings, nobody else can answer—unless somebody gets so tired of hearing it ringing, they come around the corner and pick it up. No secretaries can pick up. That's what I mean by planned dysfunction. So we sit here wondering why we can't get the worker on the phone—the worker is out in the field; no one else can pick up. That raises the level of frustration on both sides.

For other managers, GFOs' inability to move efficiently is most apparent in their internal duplication of effort. One rues the "nuisance" of having to complete different forms on the same information for different contracts from the same GFO. Others deplore the duplication of monitoring effort. An executive director describes the effect of having four different GFO offices monitor the same contract.

> Different people come to your office and demand you sit down and spend hours answering the same questions. They give you different information; tell you you have to do this, you have to do that, you can't do this. You get conflicting answers about things.

For NPA managers, perhaps the most frustrating aspect of GFOs' inability to operate efficiently is the inordinate amount of time required for the GFO to complete the simplest tasks. A manager says a GFO is "so inept" in this way that their contract is "one of the most difficult to manage." Another describes the "terrible time" she has getting clients' records from the GFO even when the GFO refers the cases to the NPA: "You have to badger and badger and badger for them." An executive director characterizes as a "gross nightmare" a GFO's taking from September, the mandated start of a program, to December to sign the contract and release funding.

Another significant consequence of GFOs' disorganization is their inability to operate effectively, their tendency to thwart their own desired results. Many managers describe how overmonitoring by GFOs results in their underassisting NPAs. GFO staff capable of providing technical assistance to NPAs are, instead, compelled to monitor information simultaneously audited by three other offices, because as one manager infers, "Nobody wants to give up their piece," and "They don't trust each other." Another manager laments that extensive GFO fingerprinting procedures implemented to prevent child abuse are "ludicrous because the chances of your finding somebody on file who's involved in this is so minimal." He argues the same funds should have been spent on staff training to insure quality and professionalism: "That's what you need; not their fingerprints."

For several managers, the most obvious manifestation of the GFOs' inability to operate effectively is the patent promotion of program instability and discontinuity. One manager recognizes that multiple-year funding can cause stagnation, but she bemoans the effect of annual, uncertain funding cycles.

> You need to have consistency. How can you hire staff and develop an organization and a project that's really going to have an impact if you only know from one year to the next whether or not you're going to have the money? That's not realistic. It's not helpful. It's destructive to the work that you're trying to do.

Noting that "anybody who's worth their salt would tell you that you didn't have to demonstrate" the value of these services, another manager gives a graphic description of what happens in her NPA at the end of a two-year demonstration program to prevent foster care.

> No more money was put in the pot. So in June we closed cases, the former director went off, workers got new jobs. By August, they woke up in Albany, put the money back in the pot, everybody came back, we reopened some cases, and went on a roll. But, again, it was only for a year. So, for the first couple of years, in June, nobody ever knew whether they were going to have a job in July. When I came several years later, it was still a cliffhanger, but not quite so much so, because the handwriting was kind of on the wall that preventive services were a good thing. And I really never went through the anxiety about funding that the previous director did.

GFOs also promote instability and discontinuity with "outrageously low" contracted salaries. An executive director whose NPA provides care to six hundred people with one thousand home attendants who are paid $4.15 an hour describes his experience.

We're trying to provide a quality service with low-wage workers, which means that you get unskilled workers or unreliable workers, or if you get good workers you're not going to keep them.

GFOs' inability to operate effectively is also manifest when their disorganization makes evaluation and advocacy difficult. A manager describes the predicaments when a GFO attempts to evaluate a dropout prevention program serving one hundred children they refer.

By September, we realized that there were problems with some of the kids on that hundred list: either they had a fake address, there was no such address; the kid had left, gone to the Dominican Republic; the kid had transfered to another school—whatever. So then there were less than a hundred kids on the list. So you have to add on. In November, we got about thirty-five new kids per school and then there were still further adjustments that were made. The [GFO] said they couldn't come up with a hundred names that fit the criteria so they had to change the criteria somewhat.

So then, if you do an evaluation of your success, what does it mean? Some kids, their names you got in June. Some kids you got in November. The two evaluatory standards—big things—are attendance rate and number of courses passed. Well, some kids you're not getting until Christmas. So how do you really judge how effective you are?

GFO staff say, to document unmet needs when advocating for more contracted services funding, they must seek information about their own referrals to NPAs from those NPAs because their own GFO offices are "too chaotic; we can't count on them." An executive director decries a GFO's inability to be an advocate for clients in ways that they, and no NPA, can. Because the GFO is so disorganized and "so busy problem-solving the latest crisis," she says they do not collaborate with other government agencies essential to resolving mutual clients' problems. She describes what happened when the GFO reorganized.

> They lost all the good people who were in there. What happened to _____, a wonderful person, with wonderful ideas? He quit in frustration after less than two years. He couldn't do with them what he knew needed to be done. And that makes me sick. It sets everything back. They waste a lot of money. Public money's going down the drain—and they're telling us we can have a 1 percent salary increase!

Finally, GFOs' inability to be effective is reflected in their inability to make changes expeditiously. Managers attribute this inability to constraints on GFOs and the crisis-driven mode in which they inevitably seem to operate. A program director says efforts to make constructive procedural changes are "hamstrung" because "everything has to go before the union." After an NPA/GFO committee develops a way to streamline the certification of cases for homemakers, she learns implementation is likely to be delayed for almost a year.

> It first had to be reviewed by the union because it involved something one of their workers would actually have to do. I can't imagine working that way. I just can't imagine it.

Other managers attribute the GFOs' inability to make changes to their continual crisis orientation: "We have an emergency;

we've got to put a band-aid on it." This orientation and its implications are clear when a GFO asks that a manager respond to a request for proposals (RFP) for a program for hospitals' "boarder babies" and their drug-abusive mothers.[2]

> I got a call this morning: The RFP was ready, it had been mailed, did I see it? No, I haven't. Would I like to come down and pick it up because the return date is Tuesday? Now, that kind of stuff fries me because we can respond, but there's no opportunity to really think it through.

Managers believe there are, what one calls, "islands of good people" amid the GFO chaos. After decrying incompetent and dysfunctional GFO staff, this manager describes her "high regard" for one office, created in the last several years.

> I think they're sharp. They're committed and work long hours. Anytime you want to get one of them; call them at six o'clock. They're at their desk then.
> Maybe it's because what they're supposed to do is very clear and they put a nice, hand-picked crew up there. I think in many ways they've become real advocates for us. They know which programs are stronger and which are weaker. I think there's been a very good working relationship so that even though we've gotten into conversations with them and discussions about certain things, and they can't always go along with what we want—because on the other side they have their own administration and the mayor—I think they're very ready to listen and to work something out.

Another manager explains, "I know there're some wonderful bureaucrats in the system who want to help you, and eventually you find them."

Several managers denounce what the GFOs seem to do with

these islands of good people. One says he is tired of watching the GFO "scapegoat" management staff. He recounts what occurred in a GFO office that had four managers in three years.

> I respected all of them, and they were all good people. They had a choice of either not getting their job done, really being in trouble for that, or stepping on some toes to get the job done. They all took the route of stepping on toes to get the job done and then found out that that's not appreciated.

Other managers note the extraordinarily positive impact the senior GFO administrator can have. One says a new director is a "fabulous person" responsible for contracting procedures being "much, much better." Another attributes previously nonexistent GFO responsiveness, flexibility, and sensitivity to this same administrator's commitment to working with NPAs to resolve problems.

Many managers believe that GFOs place NPAs on a continuum somewhere between contempt and respect. Some think where NPAs are on the continuum reflects the level of government involved or the size of the contract. All believe that NPAs can exert some degree of control over where on the continuum they fall.

Managers talk of the GFOs' belief that because NPAs do not know how to manage properly they must be forced to do so. Some attribute GFOs' attitude of distrust to a disdain for social workers and their presumed lack of business sophistication. This perception is discussed in Chapter Eight.

A program director talks about GFOs' "locking in" NPAs with unrealistic requirements that distort program development. As an example, a GFO's testing requirement for new clients in her NPA's literacy program is "really counterproductive," since the majority are below a third-grade reading level, and "It's much more important to engage them." She concludes, "It's just in the lack of faith in the private sector to really deliver quality services that there have been real mistakes made."

Another manager makes a distinction between city GFOs' contemptuous attitude of "looking over our backs" and the respectful federal and state attitudes of "tapping us on the shoulder." He explains that the latter agencies seem to "feel secure enough to say, 'That's a professional agency; I'm sure they're doing what they need to be doing.'" Whereas the GFO for his NPA's federal child care contract calls him only occasionally, the GFO staff for the same contract administered by the city are, for example, "picking up the phone" every day, "trying to find out how many kids you have enrolled, what's the attendance today."

Key to influencing where a GFO places an NPA on the contempt-respect continuum is the NPA's delivering the program as contracted and demonstrating commitment to the accomplishment of its objectives. Specific strategies managers use to gain respect and its corollary, leverage, are discussed in Chapter Five. An executive director describes how the coalition of NPAs providing residential services for the mentally ill were able to influence the state GFO.

> I think we were perceived in 1982 and 1983 as sort of bumpkins and community people. "We [GFO] know what's best." They had the Ph.D.'s and were doing this analysis, and they could produce these justifications for all kinds of bizarre behavior. Some of my colleagues [executive directors from other parts of the state] might look a little odd, but they certainly know what they're doing. I think we've gained recognition and respect for what we do. That's just an education process taking place for years now.

Another manager explains how, with persistence, NPAs "gained some credibility" with the GFO and changed the GFO's perception from disdain to, "Gee, they're doing a good job;

they're getting kids to come. . . . They could see that we were doing stuff, so they were willing to listen to what we were trying to say substantively about how we would deliver these services."

Many NPA managers believe GFOs' perception of NPAs is insufficient, that they lack fundamental understanding of what is involved in managing a program and have no understanding of the significance of such matters as cash flow to NPAs. A manager says, "The major problem with the city funders is that they have no idea what it's like to provide the service." This theme emerges repeatedly. Another manager tells the story of a friend of hers, a GFO official in another state, who hears herself asking NPA officials after an incident, "How did you not see this coming?" Later that night, she asks herself, "What has happened to me? I don't believe I'm saying these things. I'm turning into a bureaucrat." As her friend, the interviewed manager, whose previous experience has been in GFOs, explains: "It's easy to say, 'You have to do this and this.' But you get here, and you realize it's not that easy. It's always easier to tell people what to do than to do it."

An executive director says GFOs just do not understand that cash flow "is what keeps these services alive and that without the money, you can't do it." The "only reason" his NPA does not have "serious cash-flow problems," he says, is that they are a large agency with diverse funding sources. The executive director of a small agency decries the GFO for informing him on December 10 that on January 1 his NPA is only getting half as much as he expects for the year: "It was a little form letter—like it doesn't mean anything to them."

The same executive director perceives similar insensitivity by an ombudsman, a patronage appointee in a politician's office. After a second director and he have several discussions with the ombudsman to solicit her intervention to speed up the cash flow from a GFO, she accuses the second director of always being negative. His colleague wants to say to her: "It's like if you had to live a month without your maid, your housekeeper, or something—imagine what the hell it would be like and how negative you'd be!"

Many managers believe the political climate is often the most important variable in understanding GFOs' attitudes and actions toward NPAs. An executive director, blasting performance-based contracting for its effect on service delivery, says this payment system evolved from the federal government's "message," which state and local GFOs embrace, "that social services are not a priority and have to be cost-contained." When a GFO monitor tells a manager that she must double the number of case management clients by cutting contacts from two to one a month and the manager expresses dismay, the monitor's response is, "People really don't care about quality anymore."

Local political conditions also affect GFOs' perceptions of NPAs. A manager is told by the GFO that her NPA is not getting a contract because the agency has just received a large contract for a different program, and because, "politically," it would be impossible for the GFO to give "that much money to one agency." According to GFO staff, her NPA was bypassed for another contract because the situation "was just a political football."

> Here we were established, doing good work, and they gave money to a group of people who already had a bad track record and had worked for an agency that had gotten closed down. They were given the money and hadn't even really thought through how they were going to spend it, because they asked us to be their consultants, helping them to start. I was so mad. What's going on [I ask the GFO]? "It's just political. It's a black community, black community board, and they really wanted us to fund this black organization." Well, I can accept that— that's real life in New York City.

When GFOs' need for NPAs is great, they perceive NPAs as powerful. Describing GFOs as "being at my mercy" and "begging" for bed space for foster children, a compliance coordinator explains that "what's happening in the larger system plays itself out a little bit" in her attitude toward GFO audits.

> The threat years ago was that they [GFO] were going to close your intake if you were not meeting their standards. Can you see that happening now? With hundreds of kids sleeping in waiting rooms?
> Not that I'm aware of that—when they [GFO auditors] are sitting there next door—saying, "Oh, I have nothing to worry about. What're they going to do to me? How are they going to hurt me?" I'm not really thinking about that at that moment. I try to be nice, and I try and get the job done, but each time an assessment occurs of some sort, I think I am aware somewhere back there of what the impact is, and I don't treat them all equally.

Managers also approach their jobs with individual perspectives, drawn from their work experiences and their educational and family backgrounds. Identifying these perspectives is essential for understanding why and how a particular manager plays the game of contracted services. As Morgan McCall and Robert Kaplan concluded from their study of managerial decision making, "Each problem faced, each action taken, shapes what that manager will be."[3] These perspectives are also likely indexes of effectiveness: "What seems to differentiate those managers who win more than they lose is, in the most global sense, their ability to learn from experience."[4]

An executive director describes how her learning, beginning in the 1950s, about the needs of the elderly evolved into her creating an NPA to serve them. As a political committeeperson, she worked with many elderly people: "And that's when I learned how to negotiate part of the bureaucracy." Simultaneously, to place a relative, she visited all the local nursing homes and found: "There wasn't one thing good about any one of those homes." Then she became a city caseworker, responsible for nursing home placements for patients discharged from state psychiatric hospitals. She became so angry about conditions that she organized a conference. After reading her keynote address, a local politician asked her to provide services to the elderly from his office.

> And I walled myself off in a corner of his office, called the Commissioner for the Aging, and said, "How the hell do I get publicity that I'm here?" The commissioner said, "I'll give you the half-fare [subway and bus] cards. That'll give you all the publicity you need."
>
> It took two weeks, and the word went around the whole neighborhood: "Hey, the lady in the corner, the lady in the corner." And, I was shot with luck. My first Social Security case, I stumbled on a wonderful person in the local Social Security Office, and he solved my first two cases like that. Welfare, the same thing happened.

Soon after, she formed an NPA, moved into another building, "We just grew and we grew and we grew. We managed to get a good reputation."

Another manager who has been at her NPA for fourteen years describes how the "somersault approach" she developed during her original community psychiatry experience helped her create the path leading to her current position. She worked in single-room-occupancy hotels housing elderly, former state psychiatric hospital patients, drug addicts, and alcoholics. It was "frightening, scary work" and conditions were terrible, but despite that, staff had parties "where all these limited people are cooking and reading poems and having soap opera group." As a result:

> There's a sense of—in the worst situation—you can come up with very interesting solutions that aren't always writ-

ten in the books. Yet, real good clinical work is done. So that kind of background really does help.

Subsequently, she "moved from place to place" in the NPA and eventually wrote proposals.

> I was very clear that there wasn't exactly a job for me as the initial proposals were created and yet once we got both proposals, more money, it was very clear that there could be a job. So then we rewrote things so that could happen. You manage your career, too, in a way.

An executive director learned from a previous job what "I would never want to do myself nor have happen to an organization like this." She had worked for an NPA that allowed no political action because they did not want to jeopardize government funding. This policy, she concludes, "clouded your vision," because while providing services is important, "if that's all you're going to do, then these people are going to be steeped in these problems from now until doomsday." She also learned, "If you start going out for government money for whatever the money is available for, just to have the money, programs get developed, but not out of need." She concludes that worthwhile as these programs might be, NPAs thwart their primary goals and programs and may be unable to provide the attention new ones require.

A compliance coordinator whose entire previous experience has been in GFOs developed a perspective different from that of his current colleagues', who bemoan NPAs' becoming "an appendage of government."

> The way I view it is I've been in government, and I see all the differences. I see not having a civil service to contend with. I see having considerably more insulation from political decisions. I see a whole set of differences that may

not be as great as what people who have more experience on the voluntary side see, but it's just that I have a different lens to look at it through.

College courses in engineering helped another compliance coordinator develop forms to keep track of deadlines.

> I used a systems flow technique [used in designing an airplane] for plotting projects—what has to be built in what order, what gets attached to what in what order, how long does it take, and what are your required steps. That was basically the model that I was using. It worked perfectly, and people liked it.

These forms were then adopted by his NPA. He was asked to develop additional forms and eventually assumed responsibility for developing and managing computerized management information systems and compliance for his NPA.

Another compliance coordinator conceives of her job as the art of compromise, "hearing from the people, knowing what's out there, and trying to fit it together somehow in a palatable process." She says she learned those skills from being the middle child: "That was my role in the family. I was always the peacemaker, the middle man, the balancing act."

NOTES

1. These perspectives are akin to cognitive maps or, more accurately, "a set of principles for map making and navigation," since "people are not just map-readers; they are map-makers." Charles O. Frake, "Plying Frames Can Be Dangerous: Some Reflections on Methodology in Cognitive Anthropology," *Quarterly Newsletter of the Institute for Comparative Human Development* 3 (1977): 6–7, as quoted in James P. Spradley, *The Ethnographic Interview* (New York: Holt, Rinehart and Winston, 1979), p. 7. See also Chapter One, note 40.

2. "Boarder babies" are those who remain in hospitals, although they no longer have a medical need, because they cannot be released to their parents and there is no alternate caregiver.
3. Morgan W. McCall, Jr., and Robert E. Kaplan, *Whatever It Takes: Decision Makers at Work* (Englewood Cliffs, N.J.: Prentice-Hall, 1985), p. 84.
4. Ibid., p. 83.

COMPLIANCE

D espite the unambiguous legal obligation of NPAs to provide services, the effort to comply is hampered by the contradictions and inefficiencies that characterize contracting. Periodically, the GFO audits the NPA's programmatic and financial performance under the contract. These audits can take many forms; but generally, the more money involved in the contract, the more complex and stringent the monitoring.

In relating what he expects in the upcoming programmatic audit for a small, simple service, a $35,000 federal contract for a snack program, a manager describes the scope of any audit. He explains that the GFO defines what a snack is, when it must occur, and who may be served. In an audit of one month of service, monitors review daily menus, food inventory, attendance records, documentation of the income and Social Security numbers of all individuals in each household served, and fee collection records for any served above a specified income level.

Another manager describes the auditing process for the complex and heavily funded foster care program.

> Every year we get a book from the city that specifically lays out what the compliance requirements are. Then every year they come in and they do a program assessment. They look at case records. They look at medical records. They interview staff. They interview children, the whole gamut.
>
> Then they send you back a report with the things you got a satisfactory rating on and the things you got an unsatisfactory rating on. You have an opportunity to rebut what they say. Usually after the rebuttal, several of the variables get changed from unsatisfactory to satisfactory. Then you eventually get a final report and then after that you have to do an improvement plan. Then, at some point, they come in and they monitor your improvement plan.

This audit process has a profound impact on NPAs having multiple contracts and limited administrative resources. For these managers, the auditing process and auditors pervade their work lives.

> We have monitors crawling through here all the time. We have fiscal monitors. In the center, we have nutritional monitors. Every contract has a program monitor who comes out at least twice a year, goes through records, talks to staff, observes what's going on, visits the pro-

gram. Whenever I look around, there's another monitor coming in.

A manager charged with developing and implementing his NPA's quality-assurance program initially feared that "it would be a big imposition on our clinical staff to have people looking over their shoulder all the time." What he did not realize is how commonplace auditing is for staff because they are already audited by agency directors and three levels of government. To his amazement, the staff's major question about this new quality-assurance process was only, "Could you please be sure to give us the names of the cases a week in advance so at least we make sure that the records are up to date and they're in the files so we don't have trouble finding them the day of the audit?"

Even though auditing by GFOs is so commonplace that it is described as "mundane," several managers find GFOs' auditing disruptive. A manager who knows her records are in good shape feels enough anxiety to describe an audit as "a little bit like watching somebody going through your bureau drawers." The manager of a larger program describes the seven- to ten-day process of having four to five auditors in the NPA as a "nightmare."

> Everything gets disrupted. The nightmare part of it starts from the minute they tell you the date they're coming. And then, of course, all the workers get completely crazy and realize that, "Oh, my God, there're only [X days left]." Even though we've been telling them all along that they're coming—they realize at the last minute that they have to get their case records up to date and they haven't done any dictation on this particular family for six months to a year. And so they may have to work around the clock to get everything done, and our typing staff gets [overwhelmed].
> Two days before they [auditors] come, they finally give

you the list of the cases that they're pulling. Then [staff say], "Oh, my God, I didn't get to do this case. It's a year behind. I have to sit down and do all my notes." And so they come. And you're jockeying cases—"take this one, take this one, take this one"—because this worker still hasn't finished this other case, but you can't ever tell them that. So that's what it looks like. It's "and give me this case record, and give me that case record, and I need this." The day that they come they give you, "I need a list of this, I need a list of that, I want this, I want that"—this kind of thing. So it's difficult; it's very difficult. It puts a lot of pressure and a lot of stress on everybody.

Unclear expectations are another major source of irritation: "I'm now responsible for that also? As of last year? Thanks." Sometimes expectations are clear, but managers are annoyed because they know more than the GFO auditors.

It's not the kind of thing where I've tried to develop that nice PR relationship to make life easier because that's useless. At this point, I'm a little burnt out with [the GFO's] program assessment. When they come, I'm not this sweet, kind, anything-I-can-do-for-you person. I get tired of the stupidity of the people who come because I know so much more about it now than they do because I've been through it six times already. I would describe myself as a little bit intolerant. I just don't let things go by anymore. If I'm unhappy with something I will call [the GFO Director of Program Assessment].

How managers experience an audit is significantly affected by their perception of auditors' grasp of NPAs' reality—by auditors' degree of experience, substantive understanding, and responsiveness. The outer limits of these dimensions define what managers detest and find a hindrance, and what they welcome and find helpful.

By experience, managers mean whether auditors understand the auditing job and the essence of the contracted service. Their perception of an auditor's experience level affects their attitude toward and behavior during an audit. A veteran manager describes her struggles with a new auditor, who "had about thirty-five seconds of experience."

> The best one was—she came in one day and said to me, "[This caseworker] has the wrong CID [case initiation date] here." I looked it up and said, "No, it's right." She said, "No, it's wrong." I said, "Well, no, let me explain to you how you arrive at the CID date." So I went through this very careful explanation, and she looked at me and said, "Well, we don't do it that way."
> It's in the law. There are four ways to arrive at a case initiation date. The law spells it out. Everybody in the state does it the same way. I said, "_____, we do it that way. Take my word for it." We went through several of those kinds of things. Eventually, I think she decided that maybe I was all right. I was ready to kill her. She was like a gnat. However, I've gotten to tolerate her better, and she's gotten to tolerate me better, so we get along.

Another manager, new to contracted services, describes a very different encounter with her auditor.

> I was very lucky. Our [auditor] was wonderful. She's a real bureaucrat. She's minutias. She's a real picker. But she really cares about program. She didn't want to see this one get fouled up just because I was so inexperienced. I didn't know how to make out forms. She worked with me. We would be on the phone weekends, nights while she went over the proposal.
> She liked the program. She knew we were honest. She knew we were doing the job, and there was no reason that we should be penalized for my inexperience. I didn't

know what I was doing. So, she set out to teach me and, by gum, she did.

Managers are profuse in their praise for auditors who are perceived as understanding the essence of the contracted service. Many feel that to understand the essence, auditors must have run a program like theirs; otherwise, "What do they know?" One executive director describes an auditor who helped her streamline the filing of case records: "She headed an agency; she knows the gut part of it." Another executive director is glad that a GFO has no interest in the content of reports, as long as they are submitted on time, because, "Those people have never run a program."

A compliance coordinator says GFO "auditors who are clinically sophisticated are much better received here than auditors who are less so." He surmises, however, that the assessment of the clinical sophistication of auditors is related to the protocol they must follow: "If the protocol asks more clinical questions, then the auditors will appear more clinically sophisticated. If there're fewer, they'll seem less so." His more cynical hypothesis is that auditors are perceived as clinically sophisticated "if they like your clinical work," that is, if they say at the end of the audit, "Even though I filled out this picky instrument, and you're going to get a written report back from the department, I want you to know that I'm really impressed with the quality of the clinical work that you've done."

Many managers also distinguish between auditors' monitoring the NPA's written record of compliance and their monitoring, and understanding, what exists—the NPA's actual compliance.

> [GFO] is extremely strict in terms of paper accountability. They don't know diddily-squat about what we do. But they come here, put five monitors in a room for a day, and read about forty case records. They tell us exactly what commas are missing.

A program director in homemaker services, a program with "minimal" auditing, says, "They never paid any attention to what we did so they wouldn't have known anything significant about our compliance."

A compliance coordinator rues the GFO's institutionalizing a compliance system that obscures auditors' understanding of what exists. If a child, in response to an auditor's required question, says he is physically abused, even if he cannot say what happened or when, a report must be made to another GFO unit, which then investigates.

> They [GFO auditors] are like automatons. If the kid answers the question this way, you must call it in. The amount of staff time that gets wasted with these things is amazing. Absolutely amazing.
> They [other GFO staff] do an investigation. Then they write up a thing, "Unfounded." The time we spent was so ridiculous. We made a stink with the [GFO audit unit]. They said, "We're obligated to deal with this. That's the law." There's no judgment at all.

Auditors' substantive understanding in compliance goes beyond their understanding of what exists to their understanding of what matters. An executive director explains his frustration when a monitor challenges him by asking him what he thinks about the monitor's having seen only nine children, instead of the contracted forty, when "all the other kids were upstairs doing other things with other programs"? There are several GFO-funded after-school programs in the building, and he tells the monitor, "I think it's fabulous. For this little piddling sum that the [GFO] gives us, we have now provided this whole range of activities to our kids." He explains to her that if another program is, for example, showing a movie, he thinks it is fine to allow kids, funded by her GFO, to go.

Why discriminate and say, "Well, you can't go to this activity; you're funded by this one." I said, "What do we have to do—buy certain color T-shirts and put [your GFO's name] on one and [the other GFO's name] on the other?"

A compliance coordinator explains the absurdity of the auditors' not allowing her NPA's comprehensive recreation ethnic-identity program to meet the GFO requirement because of their record keeping.

It wasn't enough you give them a central folder of all the things you had. It had to be in each boy's record. It's like, "What do you want, the blood? Do you want blood?"

A program director frustrated with the number of regulations, with so many "things to count and keep track of," nevertheless says she is glad the auditors do not concern themselves with what matters.

See, I don't think that they can monitor for quality. I don't think I want them to try to monitor for quality because then there'd be a lot more work for us.

The meaning of responsiveness is captured by one manager when she says of her auditors, "They really work with me and are very helpful in terms of trying to get whatever they can." For another manager, responsiveness means "helping us learn the paperwork stuff" and helping get services for clients by signing the necessary forms. Because the auditor is helpful and also "likeable," the manager says, "When she comes I feel that she's part of the team."

Responsiveness sometimes means giving timely answers to questions. One manager notes that auditors can be responsive, even when their GFOs are not.

He called me up to tell me what our rate is—so he's good. He's very cooperative and helpful. "I wanted to let you know right away. A letter will be coming in a day or two." So we'll get a formal letter, but he takes the trouble to call and talk to us. He's good to deal with personally. The problem is what goes on above him.

An executive director explains, "If I had somebody that I trusted, I could sit down and say, 'Well, this isn't really working and this isn't working.'" However, while he thinks this kind of frankness "might be helpful," he is reluctant to be frank because "you never really know" how genuine a monitor's concern is and how what you say will be used. He describes having "found" one GFO monitor "who was really concerned, a wonderful, wonderful person. He really would try to think of ways to help me."

Strategies Within the NPA

Charged with guaranteeing their NPAs' contract compliance, managers have far more complex strategies than explaining something is mandatory, ordering staff to do it, and firing them if they do not. A compliance coordinator conceptualizes her job as being in a circle, rather than on top of a ladder. This philosophical position is a pivotal strategy.

I always try to go through a process of it. To hear what the resistance is, to listen to suggestions—because I do get very good suggestions sometimes from the people out there using the stuff. So I'll never just—I shouldn't say never—but oftentimes, do not just take that power and say, "Okay, here's the way it's done."

I feel like my job is to first take in and hear what the users need, the users being everyone in the agency. Interpret that, combined with what has to be, and then give back something that's relevant. So, I see myself as part of that circle really, as opposed to just somebody on top who sends things down.

This same manager then describes how her relationships with staff make the difference in her being able to do her "ugly job."

> I have a good working relationship with almost everybody here. There's a certain amount of respect, and I do my job with enough of a smile and pleasantly enough so that people do respond. It's an ugly job. But people still like me and know it has to get done.
> The person who was in this position was not a wellliked person. I think it was the way she presented things. It was gruffer. It wasn't with any kind of compassion for what was being asked for.

Another compliance coordinator describes how he involved staff in the design of a quality-assurance program: "I held a bunch of meetings, and I sent out a bunch of drafts, and I talked to people and massaged them, and then I just decided." When he meets with people, in groups of five or six for one or two times, he says to them:

> "Look, I've got to decide what this process is going to be like. Would you please give me your advice so that I can shape this in line with your experience and your knowledge, and we might make it more acceptable to you?"

As a result, he thinks people feel, " 'Well, at least our opinions were taken into account,' as opposed to, 'Why didn't they wind up doing exactly what we said we wanted?' "

The same manager, for whom sending out drafts is "second nature" because of his experience in government, says that he "always sent stuff out in draft before I did it, which is something people were not used to in this agency." He explains that sending out drafts "actually served two purposes."

> One was that it let people comment and it let them feel involved in the process. At least they were getting a chance to see a formal written document and make comments on it. The other was that it shut them up after a point. Nobody could come complain that they were never given an opportunity. Or, "What is this that some fool from the central office decreed," that they were never consulted on? Even if they felt that way, they couldn't very well say it out loud because it seemed too irrational.

Although his objectives include silencing staff, this manager also explains that he listens to their suggestions. Sometimes the input of the staff does not result in his changing anything "conceptually" but only in his "tinkering around the edges."

> I certainly rearranged the form to make it easier to fill out, and took things off and put other things on, and wrote the procedure differently—all because people who were really doing the work told me I had to do it that way.

In developing another procedure, he changed his proposal completely after meeting with senior staff: "What I had thought of originally just wouldn't work in this agency. We had to try something else."

Most managers consider it crucial to explain and re-explain, "as long as we have to," contract requirements to all levels of staff. One says it is essential to bring even the most junior staff "into the process" because "they have to understand what is going on in order to communicate properly with clients." Another's strategy is to give all staff a "checklist" of contractual requirements and prohibitions "so that they're aware on paper of what this is all about and they know the implications."

The significance of explaining requirements to staff is graphically related by the manager charged with developing his NPA's quality-assurance program.

> Staff felt like they were wandering around in a morass. There's not even a clear definition of what quality assurance is anywhere. They had been handed this set of vague concepts and requirements that were not clear to them. No one had really taken the time to make them clear.
>
> When somebody finally came along and said, "Okay, here are the ideas. Here's how we're going to do it. All you have to do is do it this way. Here are some suggestions about how to organize it," that made it possible for them to work. Instead of fumbling around in the dark, they figured, "Okay, somebody turned the light on. We may not like what we see in the room when we turn the light on, but at least we can go rearrange the furniture now that we can see it." That's what's helped them the most. That's what's won them over the most, I think.

For many managers, a key strategy in effecting compliance is to have an expectation of accountability pervade the NPA. They achieve this through their supervisory structures, which enable them to know if what is going on is what is supposed to be going on under the terms of the contract. As a program director explains:

> We expect the workers themselves to know what the standards are and to be thinking about what they're doing when they're filling out their statistics every month so they can tell whether or not they're in compliance. We expect all of the supervisors to know what they are, and we hold the supervisors accountable for making sure that they're helping the workers meet the standards. Then we hold the program directors highly responsible for knowing what the standards are and thinking creatively about

how they encourage and solicit support, staff cooperation with the standards. We include compliance issues in people's evaluation.

Another manager, whose NPA is "nonbureaucratized," with its few levels of management and participatory decision making, explains their seemingly contradictory insistence on accountability and supervisory structure.

> I think that our strength, in terms of delivery, is that we do know what we are trying to do, and we know if we're doing it or not doing it, and if there are problems we address them, both in terms of staff and systemic delivery.

Many managers, despite their emphasis on supervisory structure, do not believe supervision is sufficient to effect compliance. Before the GFO is involved, they consider it essential to conduct internal, quality-assurance audits in order to know what is going on, identify any compliance problems, and decide how to correct them. An overriding strategy of managers is to try to avoid surprises from the GFO. A compliance coordinator explains:

> We should be getting our own reports out of the quality-assurance process to tell us whether we're meeting the regulatory requirements. We should never be surprised by what a government agency tells us. We should always know in advance—if we're looking at ourselves.
> If they tell us that, as a price of having a contract, we have got to have our child care workers standing on their heads for three minutes a day on Tuesdays and Thursdays, we should know if they're standing on their heads three minutes a day both Tuesdays and Thursdays.

When a compliance problem is discovered in the records, the NPA's reviewer sends the results to the program director, who might ask the caseworker, "Could you please fix this part of the treatment plan so we don't get in trouble when we have an outside audit?"

Most NPAs do not have formal quality-assurance procedures. However, even without these procedures managers take steps to avoid surprises when GFOs audit. An executive director and his clinical director conduct "mock inspections" of apartments for mentally ill residents. Another manager does a "spot, in-and-out kind of audit" of drug-prevention program records.

A program director describes the quality-assurance process as a "tool" that supervisors need "because they can't be everywhere or looking at every file or going to every department." But organizing the internal audit function so it only supplements supervision is difficult because these processes overlap. A compliance coordinator makes a conceptual distinction between his internal audit role and the supervisory one by defining the supervisor's concern as content and his as process.

> I am very unlikely to say to him [the director of a clinic], "I think you came up with a stupid action or I think you came up with a terrific action." I am much more likely to do it just at the process level: "Gee, I notice that you haven't talked about Issue X in the last five months. What happened?" Or, "Three months ago, you said that you would implement a particular activity, but in this month's minutes it doesn't look like you've implemented it. What happened?" So that I'll sort of do the reminding and jogging people's memories, but try to stay away from content.

He anticipates, however, that as the review process is refined, "a very fine line" will evolve for him "between not papering over problems on the one hand and not pretending that you're the supervisor on the other hand."

A few managers talk of the importance, when assuming management of a program, of involving themselves in "the statistics," even if they have other staff to process the data for the GFO. A director of services for the elderly explains, "I wanted to do the statistics because it gave me a sense of what the issues were." From involvement in monthly, individual worker statistics:

> I would find that some people were being seen once every three months. Other people were being seen five times a week. Also, I found that people were working very, very hard, and yet were showing on their statistics fifteen hours of reportable contacts. "How could this be?" I asked them. "Well, we don't keep an exact record." "What do you mean, you 'don't keep an exact record' "? So we tried to change the form. "Oh, no, we can't change the form." "Okay, we can't change the form. You have a choice. You must find a way to report what you're doing."

The manager's initial involvement in the statistics directs her to more serious problems with the program.

> This program was in operation since the early '70s, and I think there've been some problems that have been evolving over time and never got dealt with. Things sort of reach a point, and you have somebody like me that comes in and says, "Holy moly!" So you begin to look at it.

The program was designed as a demonstration project to have the elderly provide services for the elderly. Some fifteen years later, however, she finds the original elderly staff, who are now sickly and "haven't been doing anything," are still being paid because "nobody wants to deal with them."

The internal audit is used to avoid surprises, but it is not merely a pre-GFO audit for managers.

> For the state, it's either there or it isn't. The state doesn't care why you're deficient. I care. Because then I can cor-

rect it. The State's only concern is that it be corrected by such-and-such a date. We use the quality-assurance results as a springboard to see and address why it's happening, what's happening that's creating a problem.

Some managers find that the management of this process, the enabling of solutions and problems to evolve, is what is so important but so difficult. A compliance coordinator says that because "a lot of times in this area you don't know what the solution to the problem is," staff are reluctant "to commit themselves" because they fear their solution may not work. He tries to get staff to "try something else, see if it works." For example:

> One of the most difficult areas for many mental health agencies is the writing of treatment plans. At some level it may be that writing a treatment plan better helps your client. Our staff sure don't believe it, and I have some problems with it myself. Joint Commission really wants treatment plans to be written a certain way, and the key thing is writing goals and objectives, with the objectives in measurable, observable terms. Staff have terrible problems.
>
> One of the barriers to writing goals and objectives is that people feel, particularly on difficult cases, that they often don't know what route a patient will take toward reaching a goal. They feel as though if they write down a set of objectives, that they're committed to working toward those objectives. That if the patient actually makes progress, but does so in a different way, without reaching the particular objectives that they have stated, that somehow they would be deemed to be failures, or to have done poor clinical work, or to not be able to explain this on the next treatment plan. Like, why is this goal achieved, if none of the objectives have been reached?
>
> I keep trying to hammer away that it's really okay. You're trying to help the patient reach the goal of the

treatment. The objectives are your best guess at how you're going to know that the patient is making progress. If the patient makes progress some other way, that's terrific. All you've got to write down is, "Scrap the old objectives, here are the new ones" or whatever. It's hard for people to believe that, and I don't blame them.

He explains how staff express their disbelief with his "make your best guess" approach.

"Every auditor we have has a different understanding about goals and objectives. Now, this is your understanding, but what's going to happen when we do it your way, and the next auditor comes in and laughs at us for doing it this way?" I say, "I'll take the responsibility for it." Which is a little bit of bravado that's completely meaningless at some level and, of course, mostly they know that. But, I say, "If you do it this way, then you can blame it on me if the auditor gets you in trouble."

To make compliance easier for staff, managers feel compelled to display contract requirements and performance status. Their compulsion seems to be driven by two needs. Given the volume and complexity of the requirements, they need to create a kind of collective cognitive map, "to simplify to survive."[1] The related, but more subtle, second need seems to be analytic: they need to understand so they and their staff have guidance about how to act.[2]

The compulsion to display contract requirements and performance status has to do with making things "visual." One manager develops a simple strategy, which "works," of hanging in her secretary's office a calendar of when records are due. Checkmarks are entered when a record is submitted for typing and after it is reviewed by the GFO monitor.

Many managers talk of the importance of forms and reports to make requirements more manageable for staff, "to show where we are." One says she either makes up the form or gets ideas from the GFO or other NPAs. "Fed up" with being overwhelmed by multiple deadlines, a compliance coordinator, when he was a caseworker, developed a one-page form to display the due dates for contacts, visits, and legal documents for all of his cases for the next two years. He then adapted the form for use by all workers.

Some managers develop automated display to exploit the demonstrated values of manual display. The manager whose forms led to the creation of his position as a compliance coordinator describes the evolution from manual to automated display. Initially, he distributes reports focusing on what is due, not on what is overdue. In the first two months in his new position, he generates eleven different reports on due dates for "all these crazy details," which "cycle in the foster care system something ridiculous."

He then sets up a database on the agency's computer system with staff loaned to him "semi-part-time." Now each month he generates "what we call our bible," which includes all relevant information on every child in care. He also generates reports from the same database on everything coming due. Before he began generating his bible, he explains that, "It was a hodge-podge. Different people did different pieces, and a lot of it didn't get done." Staff now say they do not know what they did before they had the bible.

To exploit the value of automated display, this manager wants to purchase the software and hardware to generate a monthly, one-page report for each worker with everything due that month. With this report, workers will not have to constantly figure out due dates, "the biggest headache," but will know how to plan their time.

The capacity to display transforms the capacity to monitor and evaluate. In contrast to the evolution of automated display just described, the manager in a smaller NPA with foster care contracts explains that GFO program assessment has "never been quite that much of a priority" for her NPA "partly because of our limitations in terms of how much we can do with it." She wants to use a computer to track due dates, and the agency has the hardware and software. However, lacking the necessary time, technical assistance, and staff support, she is "stuck."

Managers also try to make compliance easier for staff by partializing and spinning off task responsibilities. If staff's work load is overwhelming or its skill level insufficient to meet the compliance requirements, this strategy makes compliance not just easier but possible.

In some NPAs, the compliance function is formally centralized. In others, a centralization of sorts occurs through the supervisory structure. A program director explains that she concerns herself with the "more global things" that staff do not have time to address day to day, like compliance with requirements related to the length of time a child has been in foster care. Supervisors and workers on the other hand are primarily concerned with requirements for the frequency and location of client contacts.

The coordinator in a large NPA, where compliance is centralized, describes his role.

> I'm responsible for monitoring the state, city, and federal regulations, memorandums, letters, proposals of any changes, [determining] how they affect the agency, and then training staff in those changes. On the compliance end, I'm responsible for making sure that all of the workers and supervisors get their little tickler list that tells them when everything comes due, how they're doing. We process, right now, about thirty different reports that go to different people, from caseworker to program director, on what you or your unit is responsible for in the next month, in the next six months.
> I do the preliminary survey of the records for the [GFO audit], make sure that everything is where it's supposed

to be and, if not, proper documentation of why it's not there is in the record rather than in the social worker's notebook. When we feel that what's in the regulation's not in the best interest of the child, how do we properly document that in the record? But, more so, how do we make it legitimate?

While centralization can make compliance easier for staff, it always involves a loss of power and control so can generate fear and resentment. Managers are acutely aware of the need for strategies to neutralize this effect. A compliance coordinator explains the perception of the role he tried to create and now maintains.

> We worked very carefully to insure that my job was not a [cannibalistic] headhunter. I was not there to say, "You're not doing your job" and give them a black mark in their personnel file. My job was to say, "Okay, we've got to get this and this and this a little bit better." Or, "Don't forget. You've got to get this done as part of your job." Work with the people to bring them up to the standard or above the standard, rather than being seen as someone who comes around punishing.

Another compliance coordinator, in an NPA providing mental health services, is surprised to find that his not being a clinician seems to alleviate staff concerns.

> I think I have been much less threatening because I don't threaten them at the heart of what they do, which is clinical work and clinical judgment. I can never pretend to tell them how to make clinical judgments. So they get to keep what is most essential to them, and that makes it easier for them to give and make compromises on some things about the management of their program.

Managers also provide staff with administrative assistance in creative ways, "alleviating the workers of the burden of a lot of the little nitty-gritty details." One hospital-based program director utilizes an unusual employee who had worked for her for years as a volunteer before going on the payroll.

> She is the cement that holds this program together. She is seventy-one years old. She's energetic. She's effective. She loves doing these numbers things with the calculators. I don't do any of that. I couldn't do it. If that piece wasn't in play, there would be lots of problems because you're dealing with [GFO] monies and the [NPA] accounting department. She handles all of that. She's not an accountant; she just learned it. So because that piece is taken care of, it makes my staff feel comfortable if there's any problem with their salaries or monies. She has a great system down for getting vouchers for transportation. We don't have to worry about that at all. That makes for life being a lot easier.

Managers use clerical staff to alleviate the burden. One manager has a secretary prepare monthly reports with the information necessary for workers to schedule mandated, biannual service-planning review meetings. To help staff meet the required notification and post-meeting follow-up procedures, the agency has preprinted letters for the workers' use. In some larger agencies, clerical staff handle this entire process.

A compliance coordinator explains that clinical staff initially put their own progress notes into the computer. However, "there was some barking," so the agency hired a data-entry operator, who now does about 50 percent of the notes. The manager concludes, "So we're constantly balancing it out, trying to compromise."

Another program director explains that when staff are overwhelmed, she provides the administrative assistance herself by, for example, supervising students or preparing statistics. She explains that this strategy is her "way of saying, 'Okay, I'm not going to put any more on you. I hear you're burdened. I'll become burdened.'"

Another strategy managers employ to effect compliance is to use contract requirements to further NPA objectives. By finding a link between GFO and NPA purposes, managers can exploit the former for the latter. An executive director views the GFO's uniform case record and monthly progress report form as helping her NPA "stay on track." Because she sees a connection between the demands of these "awful" forms and the philosophy of her NPA, having to complete them "doesn't knock us off course."

A compliance coordinator says, "I'm not interested in compliance; I'm interested in the work the agency does." He intends to transform the compliance effort from "primarily another outside function into a process that reflects the agency's own standards of quality." Under pressure his first year "to live through the Joint Commission audit," he puts in place the mandated thirteen monitoring systems. The next year, in addition to making these "more real and helpful," he plans to have each program director identify areas, like waiting-list management or group-therapy referrals, that should be monitored because "we need help figuring out what's going on."

One manager says of the GFO audit, "I kind of like it" because she can use upcoming audits as leverage with staff to get them to update records.

> I have two times a year when I really crack the whip to make sure that everybody's got their records up. One is before they go on vacation; that's an agency policy. Then when [the GFO is] monitoring, I usually insist that they have their dictation up to within two weeks.

Another manager uses the GFO audit protocol to accomplish NPA quality-assurance requirements. Although she and her staff had read the protocol before their first audit, she realized afterward that they did not really understand what it meant. Especially concerned about deficits cited in the number of face-to-face contacts and home visits, she decided to develop a procedure for peer review of records. Since another audit will occur in about six months, she believes this process will help staff realize that "it's their responsibility as much as mine to alert me to areas that they feel are in noncompliance."

A corollary purpose of all strategies to effect compliance is to reduce resistance to it. However, managers also have specific strategies to overcome resistance. They are as adamant about efforts to change contract requirements as they are about compliance. One manager says staff must comply because, "That's their job. To know what they're required to deliver and deliver it or to tell me why they can't." But she says she will do "whatever we have to do" to address contractual problems.

A program director says that while she wants to tell staff, "Do it or go," she does not, but spends a great deal of time to help them understand, "Like it or not, this is really what we have to live with. Let's live with it, and then maybe try to change it." She works for change by being involved in advocacy with coalitions and encouraging staff to do the same. Why?

> Because I believe in social services. Particularly with the increasing reporting demands and with the pressure it's so easy to lose your head in the sand in terms of day-to-day requirements and really forget about the broader issues. I think that's a real danger for social workers.

Managers describe a three-pronged approach when confronted with staff who resist compliance. They simultaneously emphasize their empathy with staff's reaction to trying demands, the reality of the lack of choice in complying, and a spirit of mutuality essential to survival.

When a manager asks social workers to talk to foster parents about attending mandated training programs, one refuses, saying, "This is not my job to do." The manager translates this reaction as:

> "Don't I have enough to do? You have to give me something else to do? I didn't go to graduate school to be trained in doing these kinds of things."

The manager says that these little demands have to be made all the time and sometimes, "You just ask one person to do one more thing, and they just lose it." She describes how she reacts.

> You sit down with people and you try to explain to them that you can empathize with what they're going through, but that the bottom line is that it has to be done and somebody's got to do it and my decision is it's you. And that's how it is. There's really no other way. This is just what we have to do. We have to pull together and support each other and do it.

A compliance coordinator talks about how difficult it is to "keep people happy" when the NPA is always "in transition" because of extensive, ever-changing GFO regulations, "which really feel burdensome to people." The agency is "constantly" developing new forms and retraining staff. Asked how she "keeps them happy" through these changes, the manager responds:

> Not easily. There's only so much control you can have over that. I think the best thing is to be honest with people. At some point, we tried, "Oh, there's really nothing

going on here. It's just another form coming through."
That's baloney. It doesn't work, and nobody appreciates
that. The best thing is, "Okay, here are the regulations." I
even send them a copy of it. "See, here it is in black and
white. We have no choice but to follow these. We all have
to work on it together to make it as streamlined as possible."

She uses committees from all levels of staff when, for example,
developing required new treatment-planning forms. This process, she believes, helps staff "take responsibility for it," so they
do not feel quite "so powerless and helpless."

> If we join together and like a family say, "Here's how
> we're going to deal with this problem," it just makes it a
> little more palatable and keeps morale up slightly.
> Slightly.

Paradoxically, some managers find that allowing noncompliance—living temporarily with the resistance—is an essential
strategy to effect compliance. They do so until a compromise
solution with the GFO evolves or until necessary change can be
implemented in the NPA.

A compliance coordinator explains that while the GFO requires social workers to see children once a month and record all
contacts, her NPA's "standards are higher," with contact expected once a week. Recording each session "became so burdensome," that many staff began recording only the required one
session. She describes staff's attitude as:

> "This is what they [GFO] expect? This is what they think
> is okay? This is what we'll give them. Why should we
> write more than we have to for them? They're asking for
> enough already."

Although the progress notes do not reflect all the work being done, the manager decides to live with the noncompliance temporarily:

> I didn't argue, because you can only expect so much. In some areas, I have to understand what's reasonable and what's not reasonable to expect, and I truly believe that was beyond reasonable because those progress notes would become overly burdensome. That was in my judgment. That's why I let it go for a while.

Months later, the manager considers the possibility of workers' listing contact dates with a monthly summary, rather than writing an entry for each contact. She discusses this idea with the city GFO, which consults with the state GFO; both approve the idea. So, "now it's a legitimate way."

When another manager begins her job in a program serving the elderly, she finds that because new clients have not been accepted for several months, the program is providing less than the mandated level of service. When she talks to staff about seeing more people, they say it is impossible. Although she wants to tell them they have to, she refrains because they are working steadily. Instead, to enable them to comply, she uses some staff changes as an opportunity to bring in a new supervisor to provide the necessary "internal structure and support for the workers." While implementing this change in the program, she decides to "sort of coast along" with compliance for almost a year. Speaking generally of the effort to have staff comply, she summarizes, "It's really spending a lot of time and energy over the long haul."

Strategies with the GFO

Managers also have strategies with the GFO to effect compliance. A fundamental and ongoing strategy is to learn the game. Managers do not rely on GFO staff or contractual documents; they seek out NPA managers with the same GFO contracts. Talking to "people who are living it," they feel, is "the best way to learn" what is required. With the GFO, however, their strategies are to figure out the meaning and significance of the rules and to find the right GFO players.

Figuring out the official and informal rules of the game is often a complex, convoluted process. When one manager was promoted, it took a long time for her replacement as director of a preventive services program to learn, "You can't make a move without thinking of three different regulations." Another manager explains he thinks it critical that managers of contracted services "be extremely clear" about GFO guidelines "because often they're very tricky and you get double messages."

Several managers stress the importance of continuously attending GFO meetings. In order "to establish some kind of very meaningful relationship with the funding source," a manager says it is critical to attend meetings and "be very clear in terms of what is being asked." If the GFO does not hold a meeting and his NPA has questions, he requests that they hold one.

Figuring out the rules involves asking questions. With some GFOs, managers need strategies to ask questions that get answers. A manager with responsibility for a senior citizen center says the GFO "is very inaccessible in terms of being helpful." She explains:

> Their way to help you is—you ask a question, they say yes or no. You've got to know exactly what the question is and how to phrase it. There's usually not, "Gee, you're concerned about this, have you thought about doing it this way?" Or, "You really ought to start thinking about planning for [whatever]." It's yes/no.

However, the manager says, "I just keep plugging away," calling GFO staff and saying, "Hi, guess who?" and "Can you help me?"

They then respond, "What do you want?" She finds GFO staff "comfortable" with this approach.

Another strategy a program director uses to figure out the rules is to request an unofficial preaudit by the GFO, "to make sure we're doing what we're supposed to be doing." He asks the drug-program monitor, "a person we've known very well," to review the records four months before a major audit. While the monitor will not be part of the audit team, the manager asks him to "give us the kind of information we need to know right now to make sure our records are in compliance." The monitor agrees.

Other managers use the audit preparation process as a strategy for figuring out the rules. The director of a preventive services program uses the required GFO forms as "tools" to help monitor compliance. Another manager explains that prior to a monitor's scheduled visit, she and her staff review the contract and any possible issues and handle them prior to the visit. When a monitor's visit is unannounced, an executive director prepares instantaneously: "You just try to put your best foot forward and anticipate what it is that's going to concern them."

Sometimes figuring out the rules is retroactive and requires learning from mistakes. A manager describes her experience.

> The first year, I thought things would be a little looser, and I didn't know how rigid the requirements would be. We had heard that they would be strict, but we didn't know. We also didn't know everything we were supposed to do because there's so much to know. I thought there was only a requirement of one home visit in the first six months and two thereafter, and then I learned last year that was not true. There should be two in the first six months. These are the things that you thought you heard in training and then as you put them into practice, you learn more.

Many managers believe it is as important to understand the significance of the rules as it is to understand the rules. Sometimes this means inferring the significance of the rules to the GFO as an entity; sometimes, their significance to GFO staff. A manager says that although her NPA's contract requires service to 110 families, she never serves that many. Since the program is never sanctioned for noncompliance in this area, she concludes the GFO does not expect her to serve that number. The GFO seems to be more interested in the number of families served each month than in whether 110 different families are served in a year. Even the number of families her program serves each month fell below the required number the past two years because the program is short-staffed. The GFO requires that she write a corrective action plan. However, this year she just sends a copy of the previous year's because there is only so much that can be done.

> We've already raised our salary scale. We advertise in all the papers. We do word-of-mouth; we go to schools. There're just so many initiatives you can take. I felt we documented them all last year, and they're all in process.

The continued noncompliance and the duplicate corrective-action plan suffice, evidence of the relative insignificance of the rule to the GFO.

Another manager recognizes that the GFO is not going to cancel a contract for noncompliance in home visits; the monitor confirms that when he stops "batting away" about it.

> We do not comply with the home visit requirement. Where we don't comply in one program, it's for clinical reasons. We document it. If we get cited on it, we simply say we disagree clinically. They're not going to cancel our contract because we don't make two home visits. At [another program], we don't do it because people are carrying caseloads of seventeen, and we draw kids from four boroughs, and I can't do it. Managerially, logistically, I can't do it. It also is not appropriate clinically. But, the first line of argument is that we can't.

The monitor knows that. We get cited on it every year. Every year we explain why we can't. He understands why we can't, and we say, "When they give us two more social workers, then we will attempt to meet this requirement." So, it's not a great situation, because I get very tired of talking about it and writing them letters. But there's no place for it to go, and he doesn't keep batting away at us about it.

Another manager explains about "formal" and "informal" rules.

There's the formal and then there's the informal. So we'll all agree formally this is what we're going to do and then informally we understand this is the reality of it.

He then describes his strategies for determining the "informal" rules.

It's personality and it's give-and-take. You try it by testing. You find out what it is that they really want, how far are they going to push an issue. Are they really going on the statements that they make or are they making some kind of a show like "I'm in charge here and as long as you realize it and give me a certain amount of respect and acknowledgement, then fine, I'm not going to make life miserable for you."

Another strategy for learning the game is finding the right GFO players. A program director says, "I hand-deliver materials sometimes to [the GFO] to make sure they know who I am, so I can call them and express concerns." An executive director explains her strategy with an example. She receives GFO instructions regarding fingerprinting, and since her NPA has never filed the necessary paperwork, she calls the GFO:

I got somebody who said, "Oh, what do you mean you
haven't filed something about fingerprinting?" I said,
"Well, I didn't know I had to." I've discovered if I persist
usually I can get the right person to talk to. So, she said,
"Well, you call so and so. This is terrible." So I called so
and so: "Oh, my Lord, you call me back when you're
going to hire somebody new, and I'll tell you what to do."
    It's the only way I know to deal with these
bureaucracies—find a human being at the other end of
the phone who will walk you through it. I no longer get
hysterical. I used to. I took it all seriously. But now I know
there're some wonderful bureaucrats in the system who
want to help you, and eventually you find them.

Another manager describes her strategy for talking to GFO
staff when they are not assigned to her program.

Sometimes I've heard some other program planner is
much brighter, but politically, you have to go to your program planner first, and that's the way it is. So you call
when you know that no one's going to answer at your
program planner's office. Or you call and leave a message, and if she doesn't get back to you, then you can go
to the other [more desirable one and say]—"I called and
tried to reach [my program planner], but I really need
some information now." Thereby making it okay. Because
you've left a message, and the program planner can't feel
that she's been gone around. Then you can get better,
more accurate information quicker in a way that doesn't
set up any kind of negative thing.

One manager, describing the way she develops relationships
with the GFO, delineates her NPA's strategies for being "very
responsive."

If they have a meeting, we make sure to show up. Even if
they're repeating something we might already have heard

about, we give them respect and show up and pay attention and assume that what they're saying applies to us,
too. If we get a request from them, we respond to it. If
they want information from us, we provide it. Or if they
want us to do something that we don't want to do, we
give them the courtesy of a carefully thought-out, polite
explanation of what's wrong with their thinking. Frequently it's in writing.

She goes on to say that although her NPA usually does not agree
with everything in GFO audit reports and some of what is said is
not very important, "We take every word of it really seriously"
and raise any questions or concerns. As a result, she says her
NPA has a reputation for wanting to be in full compliance, which
the GFO appreciates "even though they don't always agree with
us or like everything we do." Another manager explains that
responsiveness for her NPA includes getting the GFO "out of
jams" by taking children in need of emergency, residential placement when the GFO is "over-flooded."

Using diplomacy to get done what needs to be done to effect
compliance is a common strategy. One executive director gives a
vivid description of how he "hand-holds" all "these little petty
bureaucrats," who do things that "just infuriate me."

You have to shmooze with them. That's really the word.
You have to sweet-talk them, be grateful, send them
thank-you notes, tell them thank you. Of course, they
want to get praise like everybody else, and so you try to
be as diplomatic as possible.
The way I work it, I call the person up and ask for advice, even if I don't need their advice. I ask them, "What
would they do in this situation? How should I handle
this?" So that I get their idea of what to do. When I have a
complaint, I say, "Well, I know this isn't really your responsibility, but I seem to have this problem and I don't

know [what to do]." Don't openly criticize them on anything that's their responsibility; I make it seem like I think it's somebody else's responsibility.

Another manager says her NPA invites GFO representatives to special NPA events provided under the contract and tries to "applaud positive things" the GFO does. As part of her effort to "recognize them whenever we can," she reports evoking laughter when she regularly tells one GFO that her NPA thought they were bad but realized, after contracting with another GFO, that they are really good.

Managers set limits with the GFO when they find diplomacy ineffective. When the GFO sent monitors from four different offices to audit one contract, an executive director says he "got to the point" where he told staff.

> "Don't answer any questions. If anybody comes in, make them sign the guest book and refer them to the coordinator of the program. That's the only person that they can speak to. Don't let them look in the drawers or the files or the folders until you've gotten permission from the coordinator."

When GFO monitors reviewing records summon workers to question their actions, a manager says her program director gets involved, "very quickly, very strongly, and appropriately" by setting the following limit:

> The monitor is to speak to her or the supervisor. They are to have no direct communication with workers, except with a supervisor present, and it is not their role to question casework positions. We have said that to the monitors, and we have put that in writing to their supervisors at [GFO].

A manager captures the ongoing process of restricting a monitor to his authorized role.

> It doesn't ever get worked out. It's never finished. It varies from monitor to monitor. One of them is really obnoxious, and he always thinks he can tell us what to do, and that partially is personality. It's better because we've taken a stand, and he knows he's going to get his hand slapped every time he oversteps the line.

Another manager explains that the "line" is enforced by telling an auditor "very plainly that we would talk to the supervisor if he continued in that mode." Consistently then, "He backed off."

A strategy similar to setting limits is exploiting the rules to effect compliance. A compliance coordinator explains how she sometimes handles the "ridiculous" problem of whether the GFO or NPA has "planning responsibility" for children in residential care. After placing a child in care, the GFO technically continues to be the planner, responsible for all family visits and related paperwork until sending the required forms to the NPA. Therefore, some agencies do not work with families until the GFO officially transfers the case, even if this occurs months after a child is placed. This compliance coordinator says, in her NPA, "We have never, ever done that. It's not good treatment." She then says, however, "I play with those regulations when it meets the agency's needs as long as it's not going to affect the care to the kid."

> If [GFO auditors] come, there are certain things that they only monitor if we have planning [responsibility]. Well, in those cases, I'll definitely tell them who technically has planning.

Managers also manipulate the budget to ease compliance. To avoid the problem of exceeding the rent budget and having to use money from other categories, the executive director of an NPA providing community residences for the mentally ill budgets a cushion by "guessing high" on rent projections for the GFO. Another executive director manages away the compliance problem by eliminating problematic budget categories. She explains that managing the financial records has been "a nightmare," so she decides to "simplify" the NPA's work by eliminating all expenses but salaries from the contract budget. Then, when the GFO fiscal auditors come, "it is much easier and faster to document salary" than a certain percentage of, for example, telephone and electric bills, because the auditors "nickel and dime you to death" and "everything overlaps" so "records are very hard to keep." She writes to the GFO: "Look, we have made this decision. We want you to realize this represents an enormous in-kind contribution from the agency."

NOTES

1. Morgan W. McCall, Jr., and Robert E. Kaplan, *Whatever It Takes: Decision Makers at Work* (Englewood Cliffs, N.J.: Prentice-Hall, 1985), p. 25.
2. This management strategy is an interesting analogue to three methods proposed by Miles and Huberman for qualitative analysis: data reduction, data display, and conclusion drawing/verification. They explain, "The dictum 'You are what you eat' might be transposed to 'You know what you display.'" Matthew B. Miles and A. Michael Huberman, *Qualitative Data Analysis: A Sourcebook of New Methods* (Beverly Hills, Calif.: Sage Publications, 1984), pp. 21–23.

CHAPTER FIVE

CHANGE

While managers try to comply with contracts, they simultaneously seek change so that contracts will more closely conform with reality. Managers perceive a problem begging for change when GFO requirements conflict with clients' needs, with the functioning of the contracting system, or with the capacity of the NPA to respond. To correct the problem, they pursue changes in program models, contractual obligations and rights, definitions of compliance, contracting processes, or funding levels. Managers use process-oriented strategies to develop the capability to effect any change that may be necessary and they use goal-oriented strategies when a target is identified.

Process-Oriented Strategies

Managers believe they need to master GFO rules so they can anticipate the implications of the rules and exploit their contradictions. A compliance coordinator says the biggest problem with contract management is understanding "in a practical sense," the implications of rule changes.

> What does it actually mean to implement? Not only in dollars, but in time and energy of the staff. There have been a number of times when things have come down that have not appeared to be that critical a change but have caused a decent amount of grief.

For example, he explains that the GFO originally required NPAs to contact biannually the school of each child in foster care. Then the GFO changed the requirement to quarterly contact, without considering the implications for the summer.

> What does it mean when you say quarterly contact? What does it really mean to implement that? Is the person there to contact? We could talk to a janitor, but that didn't count. It got changed, but for that year, we all got in trouble.

As a result of this experience, the manager says, "Now, I look at the wording much more carefully." He is also "much more involved" in reviewing and commenting on documents sent from the GFO for review. He says his response is sometimes "very simple": He asks the GFO to define what it means and says, "If you meant this, realize this." He asks for modifications, or if the issue is substantial, he says what is being proposed is unacceptable.

A program director says that initially she never read the contract: "Who would wade through legalese this thick? I would know what I had to do and that's all I'd bother about." But after participating in a successful NPA coalition lawsuit protesting a requirement that clients' records be sent to the GFO, she and other NPA managers started reading the contract and realized it is not mutual but "very much a 'you do as we say' kind of thing." Since then, they have "tried to build in process."

> Each year we've gotten a few more things where instead of just saying, "if you don't do this, we'll close you down," it's more, "if you don't do this, we will discuss with you the reasons why."

By mastering the fine print of the rules, a compliance coordinator finds a legitimate way to violate the rules. His strategy of exploiting the contradictions makes it possible to set change in motion and achieve his objective before what he does can be overruled. This strategy evolves because he struggles with:

> How do we deal with the systems that exist, the rules, the policies, and make sure that they are flexible enough so that we can provide the services that we feel, clinically, are the most appropriate for the child?

For example, he explains that the GFO requires children in foster care to be discharged to a parent or relative within two years. Otherwise, unless an exception is granted, the NPA must move to terminate parental rights. If a request for an exception is denied and the NPA still does not believe termination is appropriate, there is a fair hearing process.

Seeking a more expeditious way to resolve the problem of the denied exception, the manager seizes on the clause, "can be superseded by court order," which follows all relevant GFO regulations. Then, realizing that no clause prevents the NPA from actually initiating a request that the court supersede the GFO denial and grant the exception, he successfully does so.

Incredibly, because the court's decision contradicts GFO regulations, the GFO requires the NPA to appeal the very decision it sought. This process, however, is meaningless because the court is so backlogged that by the time the appeal is heard, the period of the exception has expired. Thus, the manager effectively exploits contradictions in the rules to enable the NPA to do what it believes is best for the child.

Managers continuously solicit advice from colleagues and participate in NPA coalitions so they will be in a position to create change. After recounting her experience in securing a contract for the renovation of housing for the homeless, an executive director says the situation was "crazy," the GFO lied about the status of contract negotiations. She explains why she should have expected this.

> I think you just really have to talk to as many people who have gone through that process before you as possible so that you know all of the possible pitfalls. Even then you're not totally convinced that it's going to happen to you.

This manager learned from the people she talked to, but did not fully believe until she experienced it herself, that it is critical not to be "laid back at the beginning of the process." She found she needed to make "at least five phone calls every day to make sure that things were moving along the way they should have been" and that she needed to insist on meetings, instead of trying to resolve immediate issues by phone.

Another executive director explains that soon after "the industry" of providing community housing and services for the mentally ill emerged from grassroots efforts, a coalition of all NPA providers was created. Some of these providers had other contracts "so they were a little more sophisticated and perceived the need for a professional organization who could lobby effectively with the state."

Over the next ten years, this coalition evolved into a large, effective, multipurpose organization with five regions, paralleling the GFO structure. The GFO director meets monthly with the coalition board, and annual conferences are held for both administrators and program staff. Because of its lobbying with both the GFO and legislators, the coalition has been responsible "in large part" for "major changes" in, for example, funding formulas. A program director explains that the coalition of NPAs providing foster care is pivotal in making change possible. A coalition committee continuously asks for NPA feedback and then lobbies the GFO on compliance issues.

Another strategy managers use to effect change is to get leverage with GFOs by exploiting their need for the NPA and by strategically positioning the NPA with GFOs. Most managers are acutely aware of GFOs' need for their NPAs. A program director says, "unless we really, really screw up," she believes her NPA will maintain its preventive services contract because the GFO is using these services as a "panacea" to address chronic problems.

An executive director who knows how much the GFO needs his NPA threatens to cancel his contract over some actions by the fiscal monitor.

> I felt confident in doing it because I knew that they [the GFO] were losing more than us. They couldn't afford to have a contract that provided the number of services that we provide cancel. They like it to be the other way, where they drop a contract. Nobody cancels a contract. I also let people know that I never make a threat that I'm not prepared to follow up on. I would have canceled the contract, and then I would have written a press release about why the contract was canceled.

NPAs also exploit GFOs' need for them through NPA coalitions. A manager says participating in a coalition of sixty-five home-care providers has been "one of the most satisfying experiences I've had in terms of contract issues" because of the ability of the coalition to change GFO regulations. She attributes this ability to the "political power" of these agencies because of the "astronomical" amount of money in Medicaid home care.

Several managers describe how they strategically position their NPAs with GFOs. For years before she has a contract, a program director writes proposals that are not funded, but with each proposal, she says, "You learn a little more." Then, the year before eventually being funded by a GFO, she meets with them and submits a proposal for yet another program. Although her proposal is not funded, she explains:

> They began to know us. They knew our faces. They knew our names. We became very knowledgeable and viable, and they knew that we were up there. We kept writing. Those are the things that really set the stage, I think, for our getting funded.

An executive director articulates the philosophy for strategically positioning the NPA with the GFO that a number of managers share: "Be the best agency that they contract with." He explains that being the best "buys me leverage" to set conditions with the GFO.

> Fiscally, we're going to be beyond reproach. All our audits will be 100 percent. Contractually, we'll meet all our levels of service. The quality of the service will be unquestionable. That's essentially how we operate. We are recognized, by all of our funding sources, as an excellent agency, and some of them look at us as among the best agencies. That buys me leverage. I can go down to somebody and say to them, "You can't do that because I won't contract with you if you do that."

This director used his leverage in a recent, major "hassle" with the GFO over the organization of citywide case management and home-care services for the elderly. He is a primary spokesperson for NPAs fighting the GFO's plans. Although he knows the GFO can easily "punish me for being so vocal," his NPA is one of the few agencies in the city to receive two contracts. He attributes his success to "the respect that the agency has with the [GFO]."

Managers use several strategies to become recognized as players by the GFO. One says it is essential to "feel extremely comfortable making yourself viable and visible" to the GFO. For others, the process of making themselves viable and visible extends beyond the immediate GFO and beyond the present. One executive director stresses the importance of cultivating political connections, of being able to call his city councilperson and state assemblyperson "and get them on the phone." Having people she can call is also important to a compliance coordinator, who says that when she is "really set on doing something," she uses the relationships she has developed over her entire career.

In the absence of long-standing relationships, some managers make themselves effective players by using their titles. One executive director explains that if there is something he "really" wants, he calls the GFO, because he "can call somebody higher up down there" than his staff can and because, with his title, he gets a better response. A compliance coordinator explains how he makes himself an effective player by having the "vague" title "manager," which enables him to "slip" between senior and junior GFO staff.

> When I leave the agency, when I'm dealing with the state or the city, I'm total chaos because they have no idea where that title fits. I deal with a commissioner on a one-to-one level. I deal with case managers on a one-to-one level. I go to meetings regarding a commissioner-level policy decision. I sat on two state commissions for the

[GFO] assistant commissioner. I'm also down there doing casework. Nobody really knows where the title "manager" fits in.

That was something that [my supervisor] and I had discussed—that I needed a title that could be used to say I can speak for the agency, but on the other hand, does not seem to be threatening to the people that I have to cajole and work with. With a [city GFO] case manager, I don't want [to say], "Well, I'm Sup #4," and play power. On the other hand, I wanted it to be vague enough that if it became a power issue, part of my power was the fact that they didn't know what my power was. It was vague enough. I could slip. So we came up with the title "manager," which is an undefined title within the state [GFO] structure. It's undefined within [city GFO] structure.

Some managers believe it is essential to "develop rapport" with GFO staff in order to have the leverage to effect change. A compliance coordinator says the "system" is frustrating for both NPA and GFO, and he believes most GFO staff "appreciate me because I use the approach of 'we've got a problem.'" He explains:

> They're used to having an us–them or me–you war with agency people. They rarely find someone that's willing to verbally acknowledge their side of the problem.

He says that when he takes this approach with GFO staff, they sometimes spend thirty minutes "ventilating on their end of the problem" and then are willing to talk about it.

> At first, they were in such a shock that I was using the term "we" and not "you did it to us again" or "you've got a problem" that they kind of sat in a daze at the other end of the phone and said, "Uh huh, uh huh." They didn't know what they were saying "uh huh" to until they were making commitments.

Most of them have taken it very well because they're
tired of getting blamed. So many people call them up and
say, "You did this. You did that." Usually it's not them
specifically, and they're tired of being yelled at. Secondly,
they're tired of it being all their fault.
I'm not yelling at them. It's totally different. So they
recognize me by now. A lot of them do. A lot of them I'm
now on a first-name basis with, and they know that when
I call, it's something important.

Another manager describes her rapport with her GFO auditor
and the corresponding leverage this rapport gives her. She has
known the auditor since she first started working in the NPA,
more than ten years before.

He's known this agency a long time, and he's known
me—so when he comes to monitor, I think he's been
[willing to overlook some things]. For instance, one of the
things they look for, I just refuse to do. They expect you
to keep notes on all your supervisory conferences. I have
never kept notes. I keep things in a folder for each worker
that I think I need to follow up on, but I don't have the
time or the inclination to keep any ongoing, long kind of
logs on supervision. I just don't work that way and never
have, and I'm not going to change.
But he doesn't challenge me. I think some of it is because they know me well enough and they know the
agency well enough that they have some sense of what
the quality of work is here. Now, if it was somebody who
was really having a pretty rocky program, how they'd
handle it, I don't know. But I just refuse.

Goal-Oriented Strategies

Sometimes managers have to advocate within their NPA before
they can effect change with the GFO. The director of a small

program within a very large NPA describes how she selects advocates within the NPA, engages them, and makes a compelling case for her program. She explains that when a decision has to be made about which of two "politically quite savvy" and close department heads "would make the best sense" to advocate within the NPA for a program, she will "run clearance by both." The selection of an advocate is also based on who has the interest and most to gain and who has the right connections. Sometimes it is important to know whom not to involve in advocacy for a program because some NPA departments that "supposedly" help are "not really gung-ho about helping us out."

She explains that advocates need to be "consulted and involved and made to feel very important." She describes the "skill" involved in doing this as saying, "Your input is so important. You've been so helpful before. This is what we'd like to do." Furthermore, she says, it is necessary to let the advocates "take the credit" because "that's how the system works." She says she is learning this skill from her department head, who has been at the NPA for twenty-five years, understands that the department "sometimes is in and sometimes is out" [of favor with the NPA administration] and "certainly knows, in ways I can't even begin to explain, how to utilize people and the system and personalities."

Finally, the manager describes her "they-had-to-give-it-to-us" strategy to advocate for NPA space for the contracted program.

> This space is a wonderful space for us. We fought to get this space, tooth and nail. This space had been empty for about five years, and it had been stuffed with old mattresses and stuff. We were fighting with [another department] for the space, and [our department head] fought for us. It really ended up with, "We've got the money in hand; we've got the contract; we're ready to start." Then we got commitment from [an organization] to give us $20,000 for renovation. They [NPA administration] couldn't refuse us. They had to give it to us at that point.

Another goal-oriented strategy managers use is to exercise their leverage with the GFO. Subsumed in this strategy are four major substrategies: Exploit the power of an NPA coalition, exploit the vulnerability of the GFO, connect the NPA problem with a GFO problem, and refuse to comply.

Several managers find that to get any GFO funds for their NPA, they must work through an NPA coalition. One describes the evolution, beginning ten years before, of a coalition of over thirty agencies serving youth in a neighborhood. Founded by managers from six NPAs, the coalition aims to support rather than fight each other "for the same few dollars." When only $2,500 GFO funding is available, these managers initially disagree about how to use it, but finally decide to start a summer softball league. From this first cooperation, the coalition is now a major organization—a successful lobbyist for restoration of funding cuts and considered a model by state and federal officials.

Another manager describes her efforts, through a coalition committee, to have the GFO fund mental health outreach teams for the elderly. The GFO tries to get the committee to designate one NPA to provide the service, but the members refuse, saying, "That's not our role. We're an advisory group. We're advocating for all of the city." The manager says she can fight for the service in her NPA's community when she leaves the meeting, but she believes it is "important to keep things separate" and not jeopardize the coalition by agreeing to the GFO's insistence that the committee "pick one agency."

Often, the most troublesome problems managers have with contracting result from a GFO policy that affects all NPAs. With such problems, managers feel their only effective recourse is through a coalition. A program director describes her frustration when the GFO requires, with no more funding, one additional service after another for children in foster care. When the GFO demands that the NPAs provide after-care services to children up to age twenty-one discharged to independent living, she goes "berserk about it" and pushes her executive director "to get together with the other executive directors through [NPA coalition] to do some fighting about this."

Another manager describes what occurred in a previous job, in which she was responsible for a contracted service for the deinstitutionalized elderly. The GFO required documentation of institutionalization for anyone served and "would only count the people who met the exact criteria." Providing documentation was extremely difficult because many of the elderly could not remember, and trying to get the GFO to make exceptions for those people "was a battle." She waged the fight by recognizing "that it wasn't just one program's problem" and working with coalitions.

When the common problem results from contradictory requirements between levels of GFOs for the same contract, managers also turn to coalitions to highlight the problem to get a change. A manager explains that the NPA coalition is frustrated with a city GFO regulation that homemaking service be reauthorized, necessitating extensive documentation, every three months. She explains, "With the kinds of families we work with, things just don't get that much better in three months. You really have to see them as a long haul." To fight the requirement, the [NPA coalition] is arguing with the city GFO that state GFO regulations only require reauthorization every six months.

When the state GFO is forced by the State Department of Budget to develop a new model with specific criteria to evaluate community residences for psychiatric patients, the NPA coalition is pivotal in educating the GFO about the nature of the service and thereby influencing the development of the model. An executive director explains:

> The first step was to get [GFO] people out of Albany and around to see what the agencies did, because they really had no idea. They were still sort of thinking of [GFO for

the retarded] board and care kind of model—make sure
the people don't smash the windows out and that's pretty
much it. When, in fact, there is a lot of therapeutic work
that's going on even though we're not therapists—
supportive counseling and all. Most of the good agencies
do a lot of that and really are the central point in somebody's life. They're working with the clinics. They're
working with how do people get into school and job
training programs. None of that was understood at the
state level. Definitely the Division of Budget didn't understand it.

It is critical to the NPAs that the GFO and Division of Budget
understand these programs because the funding does not reflect
the complexity of the service provided. So the coalition set up
"fact-finding" task forces with the state GFO and scheduled
joint, "informal" visits to NPAs, with NPA representatives visiting agencies other than their own.

We spent two days at the agency like two outside ob-
servers, one of whom was a state person and one was a
community residence person—because the state person
may not know what they're looking at. Plus, it allowed us
an opportunity to share some ideas. The state was cu-
rious. They were truly interested.

As a result of these visits, the manager says a new model evolved,
with a three-tiered system, based on the degree of dysfunction of
patients, for supportive apartments, intensive supportive apartments, and supervised residences. Funding levels were restruc-
tured to reflect the level of care.

For many managers, a key strategy through coalitions is to
bypass the GFO on contracting problems and instead go to legislators or the courts for relief. An executive director explains how
coalition involvement with legislators, because they must ap-

prove the GFO budget, is critical for increasing the salary of his direct-care staff in community residences for the mentally ill.

> This year we had a legislative lobbying day. The big issue
> was direct-care salaries. Right now we can pay $16,000.
> We formed a coalition with a lot of other nonprofit pro-
> vider groups to document the wage discrepancy between
> what we can pay, what local governments pay, and what
> the state pays. We were asking for a parity of some sort
> because we were losing staff to these other sources.

Several managers in preventive services refer to the importance of the lawsuit brought by an NPA coalition against the GFO
to try to change the requirement that client records be sent to the
GFO. The suit resulted in the desired change; moreover, the
impact of that change strategy on managers was profound. One
manager describes her memory of the federal judge during the
case and the ripple effect of that lawsuit on NPA managers.

> I can still see him coming right up out of his seat when
> the state's attorney contended that anyone who accepted
> public assistance—and if you're accepting a service paid
> for by public monies that's accepting public assistance—
> automatically loses their right to confidentiality. I can still
> see him peering over the bench saying, "I have a little
> problem with that, Counselor."
> There were seventeen agencies that went together into
> court, and we were one. I think a lot of it was that [the
> law firm handling the case] was certainly a most reputable
> firm, did all the work pro bono, and we didn't go in as a
> bunch of rabble rousers. We went as a highly organized,
> professional group.
> That [lawsuit], too, focused everybody on the contracts
> and on some of the things that the public sector was ask-
> ing us to do. It just heightened everybody's awareness.

Another strategy managers use when they exercise leverage is to exploit the vulnerability of the GFO. Managers perceive the GFO to be vulnerable to public pressure, political pressure, law, and oversight by another GFO.

An executive director exploits the GFO's vulnerability to public pressure by implying what she will do if they try to shut down her NPA's developmental playroom because it does not meet the Health Department requirements for a day care license. She explains that her license has been pending for a year and a half. Although the program, with six staff for twelve children, meets the basic requirements, it is "physically impossible" in temporary, rented space to meet a regulation, for example, to provide "kiddie-size toilets." Certificate of Occupancy requirements cannot be met; there is no certificate because of the age of the building. She has been looking for another facility, but believes the "bigger question" is why the city does not give the program space. She feels a "compromise" has been reached and the program will not be shut down, but this makes her "uneasy" because "technically, they could." At this point, she must keep negotiating with inspectors every six to eight months.

> One person's an expert in refrigerator temperatures. Somebody else cares a lot about the backyard. Basically, they know that the children are not in danger. The children are wonderfully cared for. There's a lot of nurturing and stimulation going on that would not be taking place otherwise.
> They want to shut us down? We will make a public hew and cry. We'll embarrass them if that's what they do. They are aware of it. But I haven't had to say it. We have said, "Where do you think these children would be if this little playroom weren't here?"

One manager, who worked in the GFO before taking a job with the NPA, says that when NPA coalitions take (or when the GFO is afraid the coalitions will take) their problems to legislators and the governor, the GFO staff are "afraid of being seen as inflexible, incompetent."

Another manager explains how a coalition gets a budget increase for the displaced-homemaker program.

> This year we had a whole strategy, and we wrote budgets in December based upon what we needed, and we asked for a lump sum based upon what we needed, and we got it. That is the power of the displaced-homemaker network statewide. They're very effective. They have very good relationships with the legislature. They're a favorite program of the legislature. They did embarrass the governor a couple times last year. They went to public hearings and asked him why he hadn't put increases for displaced homemakers in his budget. He was so concerned about employment and the welfare cycle and here he had a very cost-effective program, and he wasn't supporting it. The governor doesn't like to be embarrassed.

Sometimes the leverage NPAs have with a GFO is the GFO's vulnerability to laws beyond contractual obligations. A manager explains that her attention to the legal implications of her NPA's contracts has increased dramatically. As an example, she says that for years NPAs did their own pre-employment staff screening. Now each GFO requires a different screening procedure, including clearance through a central registry, fingerprinting, and self-reporting. With each new GFO procedure:

> We have had to struggle over their substance, because in some instances they've been really inappropriate and sometimes they've been illegal. [GFO] put out an initial questionnaire that was demanding self-disclosure from employees that was not legal. So you cannot function without a very good attorney anymore. There are some

days when I feel like I'm just talking to attorneys all the
time.

She then describes a problem with a GFO's requirement that
all contract employees use the GFO's time clock "so that they can
have accountability for where our employees are." She ada-
mantly objects to this requirement because, philosophically, she
opposes having different timekeeping systems for different NPA
programs and because, practically, the GFO's office with the time
clock is not even open during the NPA's program. She registers
her opposition prior to the signing of the contract and thinks the
requirement is eliminated, but then finds out it is not. She describes her subsequent discussions with the GFO.

I said, "If you disallow $500,000 of personnel expenses be-
cause we didn't use a time clock, it's going to be a little
critical." Then, I found out that they hadn't put it in the
contract of the program I had negotiated in tandem with,
so I said, "Go ahead, disallow. We'll sue you for unequal
treatment." So that took care of that problem.

Related to GFOs' vulnerability to the law is their vulnerability
to the oversight of other GFOs. This vulnerability is often manifest in contradictory, but contractually mandated, state and city
requirements. A compliance coordinator says that for two years
his NPA argued with the GFO over one family's CID [case initiation date], the basis on which the reporting cycle is set. When the
city GFO insists that the NPA change its cycle, the coordinator
argues that the city's CID is in conflict with that of the state GFO
and says, "We will not violate state law in order to bring our
record in compliance with yours." For two years, this case came
up in the random GFO audit, the NPA was "nailed" for not
submitting records on time, and the NPA appealed on the basis
of "illegal" city GFO time frames.

The NPA then exploits the GFO's vulnerability by communicating with the GFO commissioner.

> We sent him a nice little letter informing him that we object to being held responsible for not violating state law. That we would want them to be aware of the fact that at this point they are violating something like seven different areas of state statute, and his personnel are ordering us to violate them as well, which we refuse to do. We listed out everything and we documented everything.

In this letter, they also advise the commissioner that when the case returns to court in several weeks for authorization for the children to continue in care, the NPA will have to inform the judge of "your office's violation of state law," and tell him, "We refuse to provide false information to the court."

Before the manager gets the return receipt for the letter, he has seven telephone calls from various GFO offices telling him, "It's all messed up. We're looking into it. It's really a mess. So, it will take some time." The two-year-old problem is resolved in less than a week.

Another manager describes how a contracting problem is resolved by exploiting the vulnerability of the mayor to the power of a New York City governing body that approves contracts. Four days before the effective date of the contract, the mayor has the GFO add a boilerplate clause requiring NPAs to hire welfare recipients. The manager and her colleagues are furious: "So, don't ask me how I'm supposed to hire welfare recipients or where I'm supposed to put them, with no additional money." Her NPA serves and hires many welfare recipients, but she does not have a vacancy in this program. A group of managers then attend "until four in the morning" a meeting of the governing body "to get some modified language that would not put us at risk, that would give us outs."

NPA managers seeking a change often negotiate with the GFO

by connecting their NPA's problem with the corresponding problem for the GFO.[1] A manager describes how his belief that the GFO is "asking too much" and his perception that "they felt the same way" results in a gradual, eventually dramatic change in reporting requirements for a five-day-a-week drug-prevention program—from daily process records to twice a week to biweekly to the current monthly report.

> The requirement at one point was process recording five times a week, so every day. Could you imagine? So, we have tons of paper, and they come in here to audit and they're going through this paper and I said, "That's ridiculous. Let's work on something."
> I'm sure they felt the same way. They were coming reading records. We would pull out a stack of records like this [indicating about twelve inches high] on a kid because 90 percent was process. In some cases it wasn't even reading. They're looking at meeting days and they're saying, "Oh, you missed such and such a day." They haven't even read content, but they're reading days.

Managers sometimes refuse to comply with contractual requirements. Because of their confidence in their leverage with the GFO, they do so with a sense of virtual certainty that the GFO response will be in their favor. A program director explains that her NPA has a "wonderful working relationship" with the GFO through "a lot of informal working" and because the NPA's executive director is "very politically active with everybody." She also says that "it doesn't hurt" that the president of the board is an individual with significant political influence in the city. In the context of this leverage, the manager refuses to contract when the funding is insufficient. While the NPA has heavily subsidized contracted programs, "it's having its own problems," so her position is that the GFO must "pick up more." As new contracts are discussed, she says to them:

"Look, we're changing the rules. You're going to pay for it. You want us to do it; pay for it." And they pay for it because I think they recognize that they have not paid their fair share in the past.

An executive director gives an example of the leverage his NPA's excellence buys him when he refuses to comply with the GFO's requirement for the dates of a contracted after-school program when the requirement conflicts with clients' needs.

Basically, they said to us, "No, it has to start November 1, and it has to end April 30. Why don't you just take, like every third Tuesday, and not have program?" I said, "No, I will not do that. I'm offering something to parents who work, and skipping every other Tuesday doesn't help them, but if they know the program starts November 7 and ends April 20, they can plan that from November 7 to April 20 that they've got it. I will not enter into a contract with you that requires me to do that." They said, "Okay."

This same executive director explains how he uses his leverage when the GFO will not allow any changes, including staffing patterns, in the first month of the contract.

I projected one person who's going to do both drama and arts and crafts, and I can't get that one person. I hire a drama person, two days a week, and an arts and crafts teacher, three days a week. That's in violation of the contract because I have to get that budget modification, and I can't do it in the first month of the contract, which is when you should be allowed to do it. So I go ahead and I do it anyway. I won't go to them first and say, "Can I do it?" because they're going to say no. I'll do it and put it in place, and then say to them, "You want me to run this program? I couldn't hire one person to do both jobs." Or, sometimes, I do even better with saying, "I'm going to hire the best possible person for the position and that was the only way I can do it." And they'll go ahead and approve it.

A compliance coordinator describes her NPA's leverage and how she exercises it with the GFO when she is harassed about what she deems to be irrelevant issues.

> We are [this NPA], and we are the best in what we do. We're not some dipshit poor agency. So, we take an affirmative, "Listen, this is [this NPA] talking. This is what we're going to do." So it's a position of power.
>
> With [the GFO], I'm not always nice. Some pisher gets on the phone with me, an MSW three years, and starts to tell me about a contract, I'm going to say, "Look, take your contract and shove it. I don't need the aggravation."

Another manager, explaining that she and her NPA have a reputation with the GFO for quality work, cites several examples in which she feels the goal of a GFO requirement is valid, but the duplicative implementation is irrelevant, so she refuses to comply. For the fiscal auditor to check whether clients and workers have signed applications for service is "ridiculous," because another GFO office already gets a copy. She explains these auditors are "uncomfortable" and "don't want to know" about case records. From another NPA program director, she develops a strategy to respond to the auditors' request.

> He'll just read out a name, and I will open the record to the page and just show him it's been signed by the worker and signed by the client, and then I close it. He never has it in his hand. Because I'm not going to turn over our records to the fiscal auditors. I've never had any problem.

She also refuses to let auditors go through her personnel records: "I just feel it is none of their business." She has determined that all the GFO "is really interested in is if you have hired people who have the right educational qualifications"; therefore, she just gives the auditor copies of the diplomas of the staff.

A compliance coordinator who is confident in the GFOs' positive judgment of her NPA explains her refusal to comply with a requirement. Joint Commission, which is "the same" as a GFO to this manager, initially requires treatment conferences every sixty days, instead of every ninety days, as required by the GFO for social services. Trying to do both sets of conferences, as some NPAs do, "is insanity," she says, and so she tells the GFO:

> "I'm absolutely not going to change this agency around to have treatment conferences every sixty days. We're going to be out of compliance. Tough." I think it'll be the last straw on the camel's back. This agency will be in treatment conferences twenty-four hours a day.
>
> The next Joint Commission manual came out, and they had changed it. And I said, "Thank God." But sometimes, and that doesn't happen very often, I'll say, "Screw it. We're not going to meet that standard."

Perseverance, another goal-oriented strategy that managers use, seems the simplest conceptually but is perhaps the most taxing. They do not relent when they want to resolve a contracting problem. An executive director explains:

> As far as dealing with the city goes, I think it's just mostly patience and perseverance and not giving up on them, not letting them write us off or not take us seriously. It's perseverance mostly and being willing to go up the line, up the ladder—and I do that a lot more confidently now than I used to.

One manager, who had to fight with the GFO for authorization to create a personnel department because they "did not understand what it was like to run an agency" and how important the personnel function is, says she prevailed because, "Eventually, I wore the people down." Another describes how, through "endurance" over eighteen months and because the GFO is "not used to being beaten on consistently," NPAs are able to get contractual changes "that give us latitude and flexibility."

An executive director says he finds that by being "a pain in the ass" of the GFO he is able to "short-circuit" payment delays of over a year for a $50,000 contract for services to the elderly. By expediting the vouchering process, he has been successful in making his NPA one of the first paid. He "saves a couple of weeks" by getting the NPA to accept and hold vouchers until the contract is official. He explains how he tries to insure that his NPA's paperwork is attended to first:

> Just keep calling, writing. I send all the information back to them overnight delivery. I make sure that if I get the paperwork one day, it's in the mail back to them the next day, overnight delivery. Then I call them. What happens, I found, is when you call them, then they look for your papers. Your paperwork gets pulled from the bottom of the pile to the top of the pile.

Persistence for many managers means a willingness to "work right up the line" of the GFO bureaucracy. One manager explains that it is never sufficient to register complaints with the NPA's assigned monitor; she and her staff "always take things further and write letters and ask for meetings." An executive director explains his strategy to get approval to define as purchased in May, the contractual deadline, an item purchased and paid for in May, but delivered in June.

> I kept just calling up the ladder until I finally got somebody who was high enough up to say, "Fine. This is no problem." So often you have some little person who's

really intimidated and just all involved with "this is what the rule says" and they can only read this, so they're not going to make any decision.

It was the third person I called. It was my person and his boss and then his boss above that to get it approved. I always try to move up the ladder to whomever you can find. I find people at the top are much more reasonable and have more latitude to respond to whatever your problems are. Sometimes they want you to write them a letter, but usually they'll be helpful over the phone.

For some managers, working around, in addition to up, the GFO bureaucracy is as important a strategy.[2] One compliance coordinator says he can use "different routes" than the supervisors to resolve problems. He often uses a "back-door route," which involves calling "people whom we have a rapport with" in, for example, computer or management information units without responsibility for the immediate problem. A program director explains that working around the GFO, if the NPA has enough "clout," often includes efforts with the relevant politicians.

Another perseverance strategy of managers is, paradoxically, to withdraw or threaten to withdraw from a contractual obligation or from the contract. They perceive that following prolonged, unsuccessful efforts to get change, the act or threat of withdrawal is useful in breaking through GFO resistance. Having been "told we were the best contractor" in the borough, "which buys me more leverage," an executive director explains how he uses the threat of withdrawal to have his GFO fiscal officer changed after repeated attempts to work with her fail.

We had a fiscal officer who was completely screwing up. She was disallowing things that made no sense. She'd tell us one thing on the phone and do something else.

I went to the Director of the Fiscal Department. I sat

down with him, and I said, "Either you remove her from our contract, or I will cancel my contract. I cannot do business with you this way." Essentially what happened was I found out that other people were complaining about her. Nobody put it in those terms. She was eventually fired. We now have a fiscal officer that we can work with, and we don't have those problems.

Another executive director says, "If it's important, you have to just insist and be willing to walk away from the whole contract process altogether." At one point in negotiations over contract language, she tells the GFO and the Mayor's Office that her NPA may do just that.

I think for the people in the Mayor's Office that was a very frightening prospect and one they didn't expect. I think it made them realize how serious we were about the points that we were raising.

NOTES

1. The importance of ascertaining and addressing the other side's interests in a negotiation has been documented by the research of the Harvard Negotiation Project. See Roger Fisher and William Ury, *Getting to Yes: Negotiating Agreement Without Giving In* (New York: Penguin, 1981), pp. 41–57; and Roger Fisher and Scott Brown, *Getting Together: Building a Relationship That Gets to Yes* (Boston: Houghton Mifflin, 1988), pp. 64–83. For a discussion of "the need theory of negotiation," see Gerard I. Nierenberg, *The Art of Negotiating: Psychological Strategies for Gaining Advantageous Bargains* (New York: Cornerstone Library, 1968), pp. 81–107. See also Stephen Holloway and George Brager, "Implicit Negotiations and Organizational Practice," *Administration in Social Work*, Summer 1985, pp. 15–24.
2. See Robert E. Kaplan and Mignon S. Mazique, *Trade Routes: The Manager's Network of Relationships*, Technical Report Number 22 (Greensboro, N.C.: Center for Creative Leadership, 1983).

ETHICS

T o comprehend the ethical problems managers face with contracted services, it is essential to understand not only their "general conception of right and wrong," but also their perception of the conceptions of right and wrong held by their NPAs and by the GFOs with which they contract. When the "general conception of right and wrong" of manager and NPA or of manager, NPA, and GFO coincide, "attitudes and actions" appear to be based on this shared conception, even if the conception conflicts with contractual requirements.[1] Managers do not consider it "wrong," and indeed may consider it "right," to effect the illusion of compliance, which, baldly, is to lie, in order to benefit clients or, in some instances, the NPA or GFO. Often they feel that the "craziness" of the contract gives them no choice and, indeed, sometimes the GFO encourages and colludes in the lie. The line between "right and wrong" is crossed, however, if what ones does is for, or results in, personal gain.

The complexity of "right and wrong" for managers is obscured by the simplicity of the manager's charge to do "that which one is assigned or committed to do."[2] Although managers believe "the bottom line is that we must comply with the contract," compliance can have an extremely broad interpretation and their responsibilities are typically multiple, contradictory, and ambiguous. This chapter explores what, under these conditions, managers say they do in their effort to effect the "right."

Commitments

Managers assume a commitment to their clients when they undertake a job with responsibility for those clients. To work with those clients under the auspices of an NPA, managers assume a commitment to that NPA's service philosophy. When the NPA has contracted to serve the clients, managers assume a commitment to the GFO to deliver the service in accordance with the terms of the contract, but "ethical dilemmas come up all the time." For all managers, especially for all managers of human services, dilemmas emerge from incompatible commitments.[3] What makes each dilemma unique is the contractual obligation. As a manager explains, "The illusion of contracts is that everything is clear and defined, and it's not true."

A compliance coordinator says that for her and her NPA, the commitment to clients always takes precedence over the commitment to the GFO.

We're not going to do what we don't feel is in the best interests of the child—send the child home sooner than we
really want to just to meet a particular deadline, a particular date.

Despite seemingly rigid intake criteria, an executive director exercises his commitment to clients in a truancy prevention program by negotiating with the GFO to accept technically ineligible
children. When that does not work for a particular child, he may
have staff "just go out and do what we're going to do whether
he's on our list or not."

Another manager gives an example of what it means to "think
of the quality of the care of the child first."

We had a child [in residential treatment] who was constantly going AWOL. He was going down to 42nd Street,
and we were really concerned for his safety. We had him
on one-to-one here, and he was still gone sometimes. We
started asking the [GFO], "Please re-place him." It didn't
happen for quite a while.

Now, it says in here very clearly that they [GFO] have a
certain number of days, and then they have to take responsibility back. You're dealing with people so sometimes the contract is meaningless. It comes down to
reality. What can we really do?

Eventually, they took him back. They re-placed him.
But, it didn't happen in our time frame, and it didn't happen in the contract's time frame. So, we weren't going to
just go and bring him and leave him on someone's door-
step.

Managers also talk of being committed to their NPA's philosophy regarding the provision of services regardless of GFO contractual requirements. A manager explains, "If there's an enor-

mous discrepancy between what one feels should be going on and what's going to be demanded contractually, I don't think the agency should enter into the contract." For example, she says her NPA will not respond to a GFO's request for proposals for employment services for at-risk youth because, "They are prescribing everything," and her NPA will not "implement a whole structure that we don't believe in." Her NPA seeks contracts where GFOs "think we've got some expertise and they want us to do our thing," and are not "simply giving us a boilerplate and saying you deliver it this way."

A compliance coordinator says "a hot topic right now" for his NPA, which is under Catholic auspices, is "one of the interesting catch-22s where we're walking a very thin line" between the NPA's philosophy opposing contraception and the GFO's contractual requirement that birth control education be provided. The agency, he says, has "so far" been successfully "walking the gray line" by focusing the training on the "medical aspects of contraception," and by using "referrals and outside training," but "how do you train" continues to be "a very sensitive area within the agency."

Another manager, after describing his efforts to organize a coalition of NPAs to effect change from the GFO, explains how the commitment to clients and to the service philosophy of the NPA takes precedence over a commitment to the GFO for rote contract compliance. His NPA believes its "responsibility to the families we're serving" is not fulfilled unless, in addition to providing "an excellent in-house service," it is "really advocating" for them.

Managers have a commitment to contract compliance as well. One says she may know requirements are impossible, but the GFO's position is typically: "It's in the RFP [request for proposals]. Deliver it." To meet the commitment to "deliver it," she tries, in effect, to minimize conflict with her commitments to clients and the NPA by being "very careful to try to describe what we do in the contract [response to the request for proposals] in a way that is descriptive of what we [actually] do so that there's not a discrepancy."

When another manager's NPA is able to recruit only nineteen of the forty contracted parents for a new program for the homeless, he calls the GFO and explains the problem. His NPA does not want to be, nor do they want to be seen as, "just taking money." Therefore, he says, "If it's not real, if it's not doable, we need to raise it [with the GFO]."

An executive director fulfills his commitment to GFOs by distinguishing between providing the service and how the service is provided. He is commited to the former not the latter.

> There are a lot of gray areas that I live in. I think that they [GFOs] force us to do it by their regulations. My main concern is they're giving me X amount of dollars to provide X amount of services. If they want me to tell them that I do it this way, I'll tell them anything they want, as long as I know that I'm providing the services. So, essentially, to me, the one rule that we have to live by is that we provide what we're contractually obligated to provide. If we do it in ways that exist outside of the normal contract, it means I have no problem with that.

Consistent with his "one rule," this executive director explains that he also makes a distinction between reporting statistics that accurately reflect the number of people served and reporting statistics on how the service is provided.

> Statistics we don't play with. The statistics that we report are a true reflection of the numbers of people served. That's one thing that I don't play with. How we get to that though, if service doesn't 100 percent qualify or fit it, then we'll mold it or shape it.

The necessity of making choices and assuming risks is inherent in the resolution of conflicting commitments. To understand the ethical issues managers face is to examine which commitment they choose to be primary, at what degree of risk, in every contract-related decision they make.

The compliance coordinator in a large NPA explains that his NPA's attitude toward the many problems of contracting is that they are "the price of doing business." When he worked for a GFO, he knew NPAs that closed because they perceived the "price" to be too high—"they felt that they could not meet all of the government regulatory requirements on the budget that we'd allow them." Other NPAs "really struggled" because they felt regulations "were inappropriate or missed the most important things about the kind of care they provided."

One manager explains that the choice is over which fight to wage.

> Everything can't be a confrontation. You can't say, "That's stupid," even if it is, or you'll alienate everybody. You just have to learn to live with it. You have to pick and choose which issues you're going to fight on.
>
> Some of the requirements on reporting are unbelievable, so ingrained it's not going to change. You can argue over [one GFO's] regulations. In [another GFO], there's rigidity because the funding's richer. You can't argue with them; you'll argue yourself into decertification.

Another manager explains the implications of choice and risk in deciding to violate a contract, presumably with the GFO's knowledge.

> Any space that a youth program uses is supposed to be cleared and inspected by the Department of Health. Now, I've had the former executive director of the [GFO] say that if the Department of Health ever inspected, you

would close down about 80 percent of the youth programs. It is in the contract. We are liable for that. If anything happens in any of these spaces, forget it. We're
done. Close it up. . . . Ultimately, [the executive director]
would take responsibility for that. Whenever I'm aware
that we're assuming that risk I tell him, "I just want you
to be aware that we are not in compliance with the contract."

Conflicts

Contract requirements can conflict with the NPA commitment
to clients at every stage of the contracting process. One manager
explains that, despite current clients' needs for employment
training, her NPA chooses not to enter "that funding stream."
Many of the NPA's clients would not qualify for the training and,
even if they did, the contract is "placement-driven," requiring
the NPA "to cream," to take only the clients who would most
likely be placed. Therefore, the NPA would "be distorted into
servicing a different population than the one we naturally service."

Another manager makes a different choice. Despite serious
philosophical conflicts, she feels she has "no choice politically"
but to apply for a $38,000 contract to provide one worker for
"boarder babies." Her NPA submitted to the GFO a $410,000
"concept paper" to serve this population; "now, ironically, they
want this $38,000 to do almost everything that we said for the
$410,000." However, the manager says, "we had to apply for it"
because the NPA has a big boarder-baby problem, it has a current
GFO contract and so is eligible to apply for the money, and, given
the concept paper, the GFO is aware of the NPA's interest.

But, "Ethically I had conflicts and so did everyone else." Since
the boarder-baby problem is an "epidemic," and one worker can
serve only ten families, each requiring about two years of inten-

sive service, this contract is "just a band-aid," which will alleviate the problem for only two months. Because many of the parents are addicted, and accessing and coordinating services with drug rehabilitation programs is extremely difficult, "You know you're setting it up in some way to have the most ridiculous situation." Although she hates to be "buying into" this program, as if it will meet clients' needs, she justifies proceeding by saying, "Maybe with that worker something else could be done creatively," or if the boarder-baby problem is resolved "for whatever magical reason," maybe the GFO will let the NPA keep the worker to serve other clients.

One manager describes the conflict that emerges when "you start out with one set of assumptions and then the bureaucracy changes." Originally, her NPA had GFO contracts to provide "generic, preventive services to the families who came through the door." With the Child Welfare Reform Act, "you began to have to label clients according to certain categories of need, and it has radically changed the way we operate."

> Sometimes in moments of frustration, we say, "Do we really want to be in this business with [the GFO]?" At the same time, it's the only funding stream in child welfare. If you're going to be in child welfare services, nonresidential, you've got to take [GFO] money. Then, you have to understand the contractual requirements and be willing to abide by them. Then also engage in systemic advocacy to try and limit the really negative aspects of the regulations. Try to shape the directions that they take it. That takes an enormous amount of work and there's some success.

She says the NPA's biggest accomplishment in its ongoing struggle to "limit the really negative aspects of the regulations" was winning, with other NPAs, a lawsuit to restrict the GFO's access to clients' confidential records. Had this lawsuit not been successful in protecting clients' privacy, "I don't think we would have kept the contract because there were such strong feelings, both on the part of the board and the staff."

A compliance coordinator talks about her dual resolutions of the conflict between the NPA's treatment philosophy and the GFO's funding criteria. In one situation, she mandates adherence to the GFO requirements. In the other, she encourages flexible interpretation of those requirements.

> With the State Classification System, the state [GFO]
> wants to see how disturbed your children are. That's how
> they're going to determine what your rate of payment is.
> Yet, our philosophy here has always been build upon the
> strengths, accent the positives, reward the positives.
> That's what the whole program is all about. Now you
> have this other part here which is only looking for nega-
> tives.
> Here I was stuck. Absolutely stuck. I was fighting with
> people, arguing with them all the time here because I was
> trying to develop a way to highlight the negative and get
> all that negative behavior in writing, in the record, so that
> when the state comes they will see that and know how
> difficult the children are here. I got tremendous resistance
> from people. I had to stand firm on that one. I had to say,
> "No, we're not going to change this. This is the way it has
> to be. We have to list these negatives." This became part
> of the daily log in the cottage. So that it was just an area
> where we were absolutely stuck.
> It doesn't match with our treatment philosophy at all.
> It just doesn't match with our treatment philosophy. Pe-
> riod. I became very adamant about it, and I didn't even
> flex enough to give room. I didn't even give them the op-
> tion of including the positives and the negatives in what
> we were doing. I became rigid. Rigid in that example.
> But then when the questionnaires came from the state,
> before they actually came to read the records, and they
> wanted to know all this information about the children—

ethics come into it when they ask you things like if he
was hospitalized six months before he was placed at [the
NPA]. So is that day hospital or do they mean inpatient
hospital? That's where you push it. You go for whatever
you can get. Without outright lying. I mean that's where I
absolutely will draw the line. I never, ever, would ask
anybody here to do that. I told them that. I said—like
with [GFO] program assessment kinds of things—
"Nothing's that important, to get to that point. But, whatever you can do within the guidelines, that's okay."
    So there's constantly that dilemma of the irrationality
of the system, the moral standards of your agency, your
job to keep yourself afloat—and then how you match
them.

Conflicts between GFO contract requirements and the NPA
commitment to clients sometimes emerge as conflicts between
GFO and NPA service models. A manager explains that after
being funded for several years through foundations, her NPA's
program solicits GFO funding for preventive services. However,
at the time, the GFO's model was different from her NPA's.

The thing that was different about this program, which
the city [GFO] had to accept, and it took some doing, was
that this is a health model, not a social work model, that
we operate under.

The "core staff" in the GFO's social work model are social workers, the emphasis is a "more narrow, medical sickness or social
work diagnosis of problems model," and counseling in the office
is the norm. In the NPA's model, the staff are often public health
nurses or childhood development specialists, the focus is on
health, and the home is the primary service site.
    Despite these differences, the GFO contracts with her NPA.
The manager believes they are "experimenting reluctantly" be-

cause they are "desperate" to expand the service and need more NPAs to do so. However, she explains that from their initial desperation, the GFO broadened their service model.

> We were the first agency with a health model to be funded, and at the same time, I know [two other NPAs with a health model] were putting in a proposal; they didn't get funded. That's why the next year we said to some of the other health model places, "Let's get together and talk about what is special in our approach and go together to the city and see if more of us can get funded."

These NPAs presented a paper on the two models to the GFO. More important, perhaps, "the city saw after a year or so that, in fact, this model was as effective. That, if anything, we go overboard." By this NPA's fourth contract year, the city GFO is contracting with agencies with many different models, requiring only that the NPA meet state GFO requirements and explain "what you're offering, how it works."

An executive director is appalled when the GFO announces a new service model designed to provide home care for the frail elderly who are not eligible for Medicaid. Although longtime advocates of services for this population, she and her colleagues are horrified that the program will separate the poor, who are eligible for Medicaid, from the not-so-poor, targeted in this new program. They are also enraged that the service design is dysfunctional for both groups. In her NPA's model, integrated case management services are provided to all income groups. Her NPA will not have a contract to deliver these services, but her NPA's clients are affected. Like-minded NPAs reach an agreement with the GFO that will allow some accommodation of the NPA model within the GFO model.

> This [geographic] area really gave the city [GFO] a headache, and we finally, and they, agreed that we would

make some internal arrangements. We were not going to give up our Medicaid cases under any circumstances. We have no intentions of doing that. Neither will [the local GFO-designated, case management NPA].

The director says that "mechanically" working out this accommodation is "going to be very messy." She then summarizes her position on the service model conflict.

See how it all ties into a horror scene. From the clients' point of view, from our philosophical point of view, and from our practical point of view, it's just impossible. We're going to keep on with [our service model]. We're not going to change our operations one iota. Now, if we have to fight Medicaid, we'll fight Medicaid. We have to fight them anyway. If we have to fight with every agency and every hospital in town about this, we'll do it. I think it's going to fall flat on its face sooner or later, and I think we'll get back to the concept that we originally had and have had for well over ten years, and that is unity of service with the client.

For many managers, conflicts between GFO contract requirements and the NPA commitment to clients emerge as conflicts between legalism and professionalism. A manager captures the essence of the dilemma.

If you have a rule and a regulation—if you're legalistic—the rule says this. However, the disadvantage is you become very dependent on them. What does that mean in terms of professional judgment, professional values, professional decision making?

It is in the management of this conflict between legalism and professionalism that the issues of choice and risk are often the most potent for managers.

The same manager explains that GFO home-care regulations "get tighter and tighter." Given the strict but ambiguous regulation that people receiving home care must be self-directed, she describes the conflict between assuming liability for a person's safety and exercising professional values and judgment. She describes the dilemma in determining if a person in a one-room apartment, who does not want assistance twenty-four hours a day, is sufficiently self-directed for only part-time care.

> If, for example, the person was frightened at night or something, how would they get help? Would they know to go next door? Even though, innately, they would know to go next door—I believe that—how can they convince you as the interviewer, "Yes, I know that if I'm in danger, I go to my neighbor?"
> You say, "What would you do?"
> "Well, I don't know."
> "Oh, non-self-directing. We cannot provide care."
> So, I think regulations like that are becoming more of a problem than a help. The whole question of safety. How do you know they're going to be safe for twenty-four hours a day? I'm not safe twenty-four hours a day.

She says her staff are "really struggling" with their liability—both the "terrible tragedy" they would have to live with and the possibility of being sued—if they provide care less than twenty-four hours a day and something happens.

> See, one of the issues is I'll take a lot of risks, struggle a little bit with it, but I know what I'm doing and why, and I justify it to myself. But I don't feel that I have the right to necessarily require other people to put their sense of value, whatever, on the line.

A manager of contracted services for the retarded describes similar anxiety with "the liability question."

Everybody's so concerned with, for example, "I go to sex-
uality training, and what if we teach it and somebody
goes out and rapes somebody?" Clients go out into the
environment—there's no dignity of risk anymore. We're
afraid to risk allowing the person to live independently. If
we travel-train [train clients to travel on subways]:
"Maybe we shouldn't have travel-trained? Why did you
travel-train if he went out and got killed?" So, therefore,
now we're holding everyone's hand because we're all
scared.

A significant reason that the management of contracted services is perceived as a game is that contractual requirements
frequently conflict with operating realities. In these instances,
managers must not only choose among their commitments, they
must reconcile the requirement with the reality. They must also
decide whether and how to involve staff in these decisions.[4] A
manager explains that she wants workers' primary concern to be,
"How do I make what I'm doing effective?"

I am aware of contractual requirements. Directors are
aware of contractual requirements, but workers, line
workers, supervisors—what they're struggling with is
how to make whatever they're doing work for the people.
And yes, they bump into the contractual stuff some of the
time, but a lot of the time what they are struggling with is
how do I make what I'm doing effective. Obviously, that's
what you want to maximize.

An executive director says he signs the forms and is "ultimately responsible" for "manipulations in the contract," which
the regulations "force us to do." However, he sees no choice but
to involve program directors.

For any manipulations in the contract, we don't involve
the line workers. I think that's a real mistake. You can't
ask a line worker to lie for you or to fudge statistics.

Other managers involve all levels of staff in effecting, perhaps not lies or fudged statistics, but the illusion of compliance.

Sometimes managers may decide to ignore the conflict with reality and comply with the requirement, often because compliance is closely monitored. Or they may decide to violate the requirement, usually because they perceive they have no choice and the GFO concurs with that assessment.

After explaining the irrationality of the rigid, audited contractual requirements for testing in her NPA's literacy program, a manager explains her decision to yield to the requirements.

> I simply do not have the time. You have to pick where
> you think the most important battles are. We have
> wanted to do literacy for a long time. We made the judg-
> ment that even though the prescriptions were difficult
> and there were some things that we didn't like, it was
> better than not doing it at all. So we do it.

Another manager, who also decided that yielding to an irrational requirement "was better than not doing it at all," recounts a decision he made regarding a GFO contract to provide, at the NPA's facility, a Saturday program for children living in a hotel for the homeless. In negotiating the contract, he proposes to rent a school bus to transport children to the center during February when, because of the cold and snow, he expects it will be "extremely difficult" to get kids to walk from the hotel to the subway and then to the center.

> The [GFO monitor] said, "It's fine if you rent a school bus,
> provided you go somewhere other than to the center. For
> example, if you were to pick the kids up and take them to
> the center and have the bus there to bring them back, we
> would not approve that. But, if you pick the kids up and
> stop by Central Park and stay there for a half an hour and
> then go to the center, we'll approve that."

He gets the same response when he appeals to the monitor's supervisor and then the borough director. Although he knows doing so will "decimate" the attendance these four Saturdays, he tells the GFO, "Never mind." If he agrees to stop in Central Park and then does not, he is concerned about liability in the event something happens. Although he believes the issue can be pursued further, it is time to start the program and the GFO will not sign the contract and release funds until the bus question is resolved. So he agrees not to rent buses, and the GFO and he sign the contract.

When the "rational route" does not work and the GFO will not accept a list of the NPA's ethnic-identity programming, but requires an entry in each child's record, another manager complies the "simplest way we can and satisfy them." Twice a year, she has the recreation department list all the programs, check the names of children who participate, and file a copy in each record. "As long as it doesn't hurt somebody," she says she'll "go along," yield to the contractual requirements.

It seems to be with the knowledge of the GFO that managers reconcile contractual requirements with reality by blatantly violating the requirement. A "disastrous" cash-flow problem, with payments up to several years behind schedule, occurs when a contract for services to the elderly becomes performance-based. To handle the situation, an executive director says he loans money from other contracts to this one.

> Then the catch-22 is that you're not allowed to do that. At the end of the year when their auditors come in, every year we get faulted for commingling funds. Then the [GFO] says to us, "Don't worry about it. That's okay. We know you have to do it." What they're saying is, "On the sly, go ahead and do it." Again, in our audit, it shows up every year that we're doing it. They've taken no steps to insure that we have the money to start the contract. It's not good management. It's something that we shouldn't do, but that we're forced to do by these contracts.

The problem of insufficient cash flow from contracts can lead to a different kind of commingling of funds, in violation not of a contract, but of the intent of other-than-GFO funding. In the absence of other contract funds to cover cash-flow problems or in the absence of sufficient contract funds to cover the cost of a service, managers sometimes feel forced to appropriate funds, raised from sources other than GFOs, for purposes other than those for which the funds were raised. One manager explains that while "private money" provides the only opportunity to have any flexibility in programs, it has to be used as "general operating money" to cover the deficits in contracted services, even though it is raised "under the guise of other things."

Managers describe an ambiguous ethical zone between yielding to and violating contractual requirements when these requirements conflict with reality. In this zone, managers decide, as an NPA or in collaboration with the GFO, not to violate the contract, but to effect the illusion of compliance. Given their commitments to clients, their NPA, and even the GFO, some managers decide that, given the realities they face, the only way to manage a program is to violate the contract, but record what occurs as if it were in compliance. An executive director says he reports activities as specified in the contract, even if they are not.

> Let's say, we're scheduled to have this activity, and I can't hire a person for that activity, but the kids say, "Oh, we'd like to have this [other] activity." I'll go ahead and hire that activity, and we'll just report it as the other activity. I have no qualms about that because I'm providing the service, and my sense is they're making me do that because, really, what I should just have to do is call them up, tell them I'm doing it, and write a letter. I'm still getting the service that they want—youth involvement.

A GFO requires daily statistics on the number of different children served. An executive director explains that he has an accurate count of children served in each activity, but many participate in more than one. He has neither the time nor the staff to prepare an unduplicated count. Therefore, until he had a computer to generate the statistics, he says, "I just made them up."

In a variation of recording as if in compliance, the same executive director includes outreach worker positions in a contract for a truancy prevention program, without disclosing that the workers also teach in a similar program partly funded by another GFO. Although his objective is to use different funding sources to create a comprehensive program, he does not believe the GFO will approve of what he actually does. Therefore, he writes in the contract proposal:

> "They're going to do individual work with the kids in the classroom; they're going to make home visits; they're going to make the referrals for the kids who have problems." All that is real. I just don't say, "They're also considered a teacher and have to teach two classes during the day."

He believes his risk in doing this is minimal since the GFO monitors "never, ever, ask to see this program or to meet these people," nor are they interested in the employment counseling and college preparation contract components. The monitors are "happy" to see only the contracted after-school program, "with little kids getting homework help and doing arts and crafts and playing basketball," since "that's what they think of as [a GFO] program."

Another manager believes that reporting expenditures for other than the contracted program as though they are in compliance is "part of the game." She explains that this practice is not a dilemma, because "everybody has to do that."

> We run the program for the first six months with almost no OTPS [other than personal services]. We don't spend

money. We don't have any money to spend. We've got to wait till the money comes in. So we stockpile office supplies and our activity group supplies as much as possible, knowing that cycle. We bill against the other contracts where we can. It's generic categories so if I have to buy snacks I can. Some of the funding streams are quite flexible so you can do it. And that flexibility is critical.

She then explains that only if she were "to buy supplies at the cost of hiring personnel" would this diversion of funds be a dilemma because, "You can run it all without any supplies if you had to, if you had decent people."

Let's say, for instance, that we were very tight in a series of programs, so I decided to keep a position open in drop-out prevention and take that $20,000 in accruals and put it in the supply category so I could buy supplies for all. That's a hypothetical. I would have problems doing that. If we can't fill the position, which of course a lot of times you can't, that's one thing. To consciously leave it open, we haven't had to do that. I mean it's not inconceivable that we couldn't. That would be a very difficult decision because I would know that I was reducing staff and that was reducing service delivery. I would get by the contract because, particularly in that contract, the way we've got it structured, we deliver.

Another way managers effect the illusion of compliance is to relabel an existing practice in the NPA as the practice required under the contract. A compliance coordinator explains:

Another trick is to take—and everybody in the world does it—to take existing processes and relabel them as part of the quality-assurance process. So that, for example, we're required to do patient care monitoring, which basically means looking at cases that are problematic and subjecting them to scrutiny that's outside the normal run of supervision. Everybody does that.

So you take the existing case consultations, and you make up a form for it, and you say, "Okay, whenever a worker says to the office director or the chief psychiatrist or whatever it is, 'I'm running into real problems with this case, would you please give me a consult?' would you please check off a very simple form?" Presto, chango, we're done case review monitoring. That'll get refined and made more sophisticated over time, but that's another way to try to keep there from being a consult stretch.

Another manager has staff change roles during meetings and become another committee to effect the appearance of compliance.

We're in the Executive Committee. I say, "Now, we're going to need a Quality Assurance Committee. Okay, everybody." We try to streamline as much as we can, because obviously the regulations just keep tumbling in.

A program director relates a more complex relabeling process but says "there's no question in my mind that we should do it." Her NPA plans to take a program 100 percent funded by one GFO and have staff in that program supervise a program funded by another GFO by relabeling their unpaid overtime in one program as paid time in the other program.

What we're going to do is work out very detailed time schedules. And every amount of time that a couple of supervisory people spend on this program, they'll clock it in some way, indicate what they were doing, and make sure that their hours for the week are thirty-five hours plus that, so that if [the original GFO] comes in, they can't say,

"Hey, how come you're using our dollars to serve somebody else in the program?" And, that's crazy. Absolutely crazy.

Is it a problem? It's going to be a major problem. It's going to be a nightmare. But it's trying to do something within crazy guidelines. We do it because we want to provide service to the community.

Managers also effect the appearance of compliance by orchestrating the audit process. An executive director describes how he prepares for the GFO inspection of apartments for the mentally ill.

They'll want to see them neat, clean. They want to see food in the refrigerator. Like who's got an apartment that looks like that? So we make sure that it's neat, clean.

After being faulted in an audit for insufficient client contacts in a number of cases, a manager tries to have all such cases, if they are to be closed soon anyway, closed before the next audit. For two years, she has heard from other NPAs that the GFO uses only July statistics to select cases for audit. So she says to her staff,

"Better look at your cases. If they're on the caseload in July, then they're free game for audit, and if they're not, they're probably not going to be picked up this go-around."

NPAs sometimes effect the illusion of compliance in collaboration with GFOs. The conflict between contractual requirements and reality is frequently so blatant that collaboration appears to be necessary if the service is to be provided.

There's a lot of semantics in the game. I use the word "game" very specifically. It's changed very little in the way we do things here, as much as the way we word things.

A compliance coordinator explains how his NPA records punishment of children so it will be acceptable to the GFO, which essentially mandates rewarding positive behavior and ignoring negative behavior.

> State laws are very, very picky on what you can and cannot do. And part of it is how you word it. You do not deprive a person of his allowance—you do not give them the bonus. You cannot ground a child because it denies them socialization. On the other hand, if you don't allow them two hours of time out, above and beyond their eight o'clock, that's okay. Rather than saying, "You're normally out till ten, but because you were bad you can only go out to eight today," you say, "You're only allowed till eight, but because you've been good, you can stay out till ten tonight." Same difference.

He explains how he learns about this semantics game.

> Getting burned. Looking at my hand and wondering, "Okay, now the city slapped me or the state slapped me for doing that wrong. What did they cite? They cited this. What does that mean? What is the wording? Is there any other way around it? Okay, well, next time we'll word it this way and see what happens. Oh, they accepted it that way. Okay."

Then he describes how he involves the entire NPA staff.

> We approach it as a game with the case managers, with the supervisors. We say, "Look, we're working with you on a clinical level. You get at least an hour's supervision, if not two hours supervision, a week, plus group, plus in-service training, plus monitoring. So we know what you're doing, plus your records are read. We know that

clinically we're doing what we want for these children, which is what's in their best interest. Now, how do we play the game so the city doesn't sit there and say we're doing it wrong?" We literally put it out in in-service training: it's a semantics game. How do you word it to get as much credit as possible?

To give you an idea. If you sit there and go out to a house and take the child from that house to the natural parents' house, deliver them, and then come back to the office, talking all along to everybody involved—that's one interview. You sit there and you write it as, "I went to the house. At the house I interviewed the foster mother and discussed this. I also talked to the child and discussed X, Y, Z. During the drive, I further interviewed the child and talked about X, Y, Z, and R. We arrived at the natural parents' house, and at the natural parents' house we talked about A, B, C, and D, and we discussed with the child D, E, and maybe some of A." Putting it in that way, listing out your locations, you've now got instead of one interview with the foster parent, with the child, the natural parent—you've got an in-house interview with the foster parent, an in-house interview with the child, an out-of-house interview with the child, an in-house interview with the natural parent, and an interview with the child in the home of the natural parent. So you're now up to seven interviews instead of three. Just by how it's worded and by defining where you were each part of the way. It's a semantics game.

If staff are bothered with the "pickiness" of the GFO requirements or with the necessity of playing the game, he has a ready response.

We explain how the law works that you have to interview the parents, natural parents in the home, X number of times, as well as total interviews. Foster parents have to be interviewed so many times at their houses, as well as total. The child has to be interviewed so many times at each of those places, plus total. By wording it this way, you get credit for each of these areas. We say, "Think of it like a jigsaw puzzle. You've got X, Y, and Z. You've got all these little pieces that you've got to put together for a jigsaw puzzle to make it complete. They've given you all of these little pieces that you've got to do. If you happen to have four of them that came out of the box together, why not put them in together? Do you want to take them apart? Is your purpose having fun with filling out the thing or is your purpose getting the puzzle done? You've got better things to do with your time.

Asked if the GFO acknowledges the game aspect of compliance, this manager responds, "Sure, [GFO] program assessment coordinators and supervisors sit there and say, 'You haven't learned to play the game yet on this one.'" After being penalized for too many transfers of children between foster homes, he says, "We now play the game." He is coached by the supervisor of GFO audits, "the nitpicky unit" of staff who "keep themselves in business by finding fault."

The [GFO] supervisor said, "You haven't learned to play the game yet. You've got to realize when you transfer a sibling group, one child has a problem. The rest are transferred to keep the sibling group together; that way they're exempt from being credited against you—it's only one [transfer], instead of however many children there are. You've just got to word it right."

Taking the supervisor's advice, the manager appeals the audit and receives a much better rating. He believes "the concept behind what they're asking for has reasonably good clinical validity." However:

The way they go about monitoring it, requiring the documentation, it's now turned into a one-upmanship game: I can document it better than you can find the errors. There are some agencies that may need to have this type of review done. There are many agencies that are at the stage now that it's, "Okay, who can play the game better? Who can read the mistakes between the lines? Okay, you-didn't-dot-this-'i'-so-it-doesn't-count routine." That's what gets us frustrated because we're using so much time to play the game, rather than provide services to the children.

An executive director relates another version of the semantics game. The city GFO is reimbursed by the state GFO for 75 percent of the cost of her NPA's contract if the clients served are "Mandated" (at risk of foster placement); if the clients are "Optional" (not at risk), there is no reimbursement. Before she knows this and learns she must collaborate with the GFO to effect the illusion of compliance, she labels a family "Optional" and receives a call "so fast" from the GFO, asking "Can't they be 'Mandated'?"

I said, "Well, sure, they could be maybe; if things really got much worse, the kid could be removed. But, we didn't think it was a factor."
"Oh, please put 'Mandated.' Change it."
And, I said, "Why?"
"Because if it's 'Optional,' it doesn't count."

When a manager tells the GFO, which has contracted with the NPA to provide an intergenerational program, that he wants to take the participants on a bus trip, the GFO asks, "Who's paying for the seniors?" The manager replies, "But it's one bus." The GFO says they are only funding the youth portion of the program; senior citizens cannot go in a bus wholly funded by the GFO.

> We had to go down and fudge in terms of how we're
> going to take a bus load of kids to, let's say, Hershey,
> Pennsylvania. Then say, "Fine, we will only take the kids.
> There're twenty kids that would be on a bus that can seat
> fifty. We're taking half a bus." So, they were willing to ac-
> cept that.

He explains that even though the GFO monitor knows that the
NPA is going to take the seniors in the empty seats on the bus,
"he just wanted to hear" that the GFO is only funding the bus for
the youth.

Another manager explains what the city GFO advises her to
do when the state GFO eliminates funding for tutoring and recreation.

> We call it "respite services" or "engagement services."
> Again, [the city GFO] said, "Call it something else." They
> know what it's going for.

An unusual variation of GFO and NPA collaboration to effect
the illusion of compliance is reported by one executive director.
The GFO paid him on a GFO "janitor line" while he was developing his NPA to serve the mentally ill in the community. Another
manager says, "I work really in two sets of figures—one is the
real salaries we pay and one is what my budget shows." She says
the GFO is aware of the discrepancy, but suspects they collaborate with her because she has enough staff turnover that she does
not exceed the total annual salary budget.

A program director talks about what happens when "funding
guidelines are not set up in terms of what the program actually is
funded to do." When the GFO asks for "creative, innovative"
proposals for services for the deinstitutionalized mentally ill,
they receive and contract for "all kinds of interesting models."
Then, regardless of the model, the GFO tells the NPAs, "Okay,

you get funded under case management; you get funded under day treatment; you get funded under this."

People said, "Wait a minute. How do we fit within these guidelines?"
That was an ongoing struggle. We found ways to count it under certain things. For example, one worker's time and everything she did got logged under one thing called case management—regardless of what she was doing. Everything she was doing fit within that rubric. Like she would do groups, but they would be in terms of entitlements or resources and so forth.
You find all kinds of ways to maneuver. It's not that you can't tell them you're going to do it, but you figure out how to do it.

The GFO's response to her telling them she is going to create the illusion of compliance is, "Okay. Call it whatever you want."

My sense is that most government contracts don't really care how you do it as long as you can justify it to them because then they can justify it to somebody.

NOTES

1. Barbara Ley Toffler, *Tough Choices: Managers Talk Ethics* (New York: John Wiley and Sons, 1986), p. 10. For discussions of ethical behavior in social work, see Charles S. Levy, *Social Work Ethics* (New York: Human Sciences Press, 1976); Frederic G. Reamer, *Ethical Dilemmas in Social Service* (New York: Columbia University Press, 1982); and Margaret L. Rhodes, *Ethical Dilemmas in Social Work Practice* (Boston: Routledge and Kegan Paul, 1986).
2. Charles S. Levy, *Guide to Ethical Decisions and Actions for Social Service Administrators: A Handbook for Managerial Personnel* (New York: The Haworth Press, 1982), p. 66.

3. Toffler, *Tough Choices: Managers Talk Ethics*, p. 17. In her report of empirical research on business managers' ethical "tough choices," Toffler notes: "Competing claims—being 'pulled in two or more directions'—was frequently cited as an identifying feature of ethical situations."

4. None of these managers speaks of involving the NPA board of directors in these decisions. The extent to which individual managers make these kinds of choices alone and their reasons for doing so merit further research. Certainly, if the management of contracted services requires unacknowledged deceptive practices, managers' decisions do not meet the "test of publicity." "Moral justification . . . cannot be exclusive or hidden; it has to be capable of being made public." See Sissela Bok, *Lying: Moral Choice in Public and Private Life* (New York: Vintage Books, 1978), pp. 95–112.

CHAPTER SEVEN

ACCOUNTABILITY

Beyond what managers say they do to effect compliance, change, or ethical practice is their perception of the meaning and impact of accountability for both NPAs and GFOs. This accountability, while theoretically unilateral, is mutual, reflecting the symbiotic relationship between GFOs and NPAs.[1] Each needs the other, just as any game to be played requires an opponent. Therefore, understanding NPAs' accountability to GFOs requires understanding the interactive nature of that accountability.[2]

A manager succinctly states her perception that GFOs view contracted services as GFO-controlled.

> Another problem in contracting with the city is that
> you're not truly contracting with them as two equal par-
> ties. The city says, "This is the game. If you want to get in
> it, sign our contract."

Another manager is incredulous at how frighteningly explicit the
superior legal power of the GFO is made in contracts.

> What is in the boilerplates of these contracts is unbeliev-
> able. It's unbelievable. We have no standing in any of
> these relationships. We are at total risk. They could cancel
> the contract—just like that. We fight the most difficult as-
> pects of the boilerplate, but when I read the boilerplates,
> they scare the living daylights out of me.

This manager explains that what she finds most objectionable are
the boilerplate clauses giving the GFO the "right to ask for any
information whenever they decide they want it, in whatever
form they want it, and that if we don't comply, they can cancel
the contract." One GFO, she says, has changed the reporting
system twice in the first two years of the contract.

> Public agencies take action. They never think about the
> cost to the contractor of the actions or of the require-
> ments. It's just not a question that ever enters their mind.

An executive director grasps the GFO's view of their power
when, after his NPA has been awarded a contract, he experiences
their "crazy" handling of the contract execution.

> They dragged it out at the end, even knowing that we
> were suffering and that we were having severe cash-flow
> problems. They didn't care. That was of no consideration
> to them whatsoever. They said, "These are the problems
> with temporary organizations when they're trying to affix
> themselves to permanent organizations."

When the contracted program design does not address the cause of the problem, a manager says the GFO's program accountability efforts seem trivial. He describes the GFO's truancy prevention contract as "an add-on program," based on the incorrect assumption that "all the problems are the kids' problems," that poor attendance and performance are not related to "how the system works."

> So the system's generating more and more dropouts and truants while you're over here trying to do something. The problem is it's going to last three to five years as a program per se and then what's going to happen? You've helped those kids that are coming through while you're there. Then you're gone. The system's going to be just the same.

The GFO may perceive itself (or, perhaps more accurately, legally position itself) as all powerful. However, it is not, in part because NPAs' perspective on their own accountability is quite different from that of GFOs. And that difference in perspective affects the way NPAs perceive and play the game and, therefore, the power distribution in the game itself.

A manager explains that GFOs perceive themselves broadly, as using NPAs for GFOs' purposes, but that NPAs perceive GFOs' role narrowly, as a funder of NPAs' purposes.

> I think obviously from the [GFOs'] perspective, they are obsessed with accountability, and they do view the contract agencies as working for them, as their agents in delivery of service. So they would emphasize their power in the contracting relationship, the appropriateness of their exercise of that power. From a contract agency point of view, the public funds enable us to do what we are incorporated to do, and it's enabling and facilitating. So to oversimplify it, they view their role in the broadest, and we view it in the narrowest. Somewhere in that, we have to work it out.

I think their job is to get us the money and let us do what we do and hassle us as little as possible. Insure that we spend the public money—I'm not saying don't make sure that we do what we're supposed to be doing, but do it in a way that is appropriate, that doesn't impact upon our service, and with a consciousness of the cost of accountability. They just think that we work for them.

She says the most significant, "enraging" manifestation of this difference in perspective occurs when GFOs demand increased service or increased accountability with no increase in funding and consider NPAs "self-serving" for asking for an increase.

NPAs' perspective on their accountability is quite different from that of GFOs' in another fundamental way. Employees hired under a contract, even if they are 100-percent funded through that contract, typically view themselves as NPA, not GFO, employees. As one manager explains:

The monies come in from these two grants, but we are [NPA] employees, whose funding source is [the GFO]. That's not unusual in a large system. Therefore, my staff are [NPA union] employees. They have [NPA union] standard salaries. We're required to participate in [NPA meetings]. I do [NPA] evaluations on my staff, with a six-month probationary period on my staff that's required for all [NPA staff] in all departments. Ultimately, my boss, if there were a management dilemma, could probably decide to switch staff from my program to another program and take other staff into my program, at management's prerogative. I mean, this is [NPA] staff.

That these GFO-funded NPA staff consider themselves NPA employees both reflects and heightens NPAs' perspective on their own accountability. As one manager explains, her NPA has its own "mission" and "programmatic concept," and the contracted services game is just imposed on that. Her objective is to be accountable to her NPA's purpose and to make the game work for the NPA—to achieve its purpose.

> Whatever I do contractually is driven by a programmatic concept. The most important thing is a sense of what the mission or the direction and the purpose of the particular programs are. Why do we want to do this? Why is this important and what are we trying to achieve? Can we do that? And then, this is the jungle gym that they're [GFO] going to put over us that we have to try to do it within.
>
> Even though a lot of my time is spent on the contractual stuff, the time that's spent is insuring that the contractual stuff enables the program to do what is needed or what is wanted. Because you not only need to conform to contractual requirements, you need to conform with why people want to work with [the NPA] and why [the NPA] started doing this in the first place. In a sense, a coincidence between that purpose and what we're doing is the most important thing, and then the conformance with the contract is secondary, which is why we have never gone after money just to go after money.

Managers also believe they hold NPAs to a higher standard of accountability than GFOs. An executive director says of contract requirements, "We would expect to exceed those minimum standards." Another manager says the GFO auditors "think we're fine" administratively, but she does not: "There are a lot of ways it could be better." Again and again managers express in different ways what one states simply, "We're concerned with more than paper compliance; we're committed to providing a very high-quality, professional service, and we don't consider that complying with contracts is sufficient." Because her NPA wants to meet higher standards, to have "the freedom to do the thing the way we think it should be done," an executive director says they must raise the funds to enable them to do so and be "very self-critical" and "very connected to other groups that keep you professionally on your toes."

Several managers talk about their desire and efforts to change the game by seizing the initiative for accountability from GFOs. One maintains social workers "should have led the way" in defining accountability; as a result of not doing so, "we're being held so damn accountable now," when "much more flexibility" is required to deliver effective services. She is particularly concerned with GFOs' using case management to provide a lot of "cheap" units of service and believes it is "deprofessionalizing social work" and "should have never been allowed to happen." She fears that if social workers do not start influencing GFO definitions of accountability in case management, the service will be no more than the equivalent of, "You need a haircut? Here, why don't you call Joe down the street? He does a good job."

Another manager says the "young upstarts" in preventive services "came in kind of hot shot," determined to "prove their programs were valuable." In effect, by trying to seize the initiative for accountability from the GFO, they seek "to avoid" what happened with foster care, which was severely criticized and then "had a lot of things laid on them" by the GFO. She is involved with an NPA coalition's effort to work with the GFO to determine what data is useful to collect and how it should be collected. As part of this effort, NPAs have been struggling to develop a self-evaluation system that can demonstrate value to the GFO and legislators.

> I know what their money's buying. But I don't think what I know is being translated into the right kind of data to have meaning for legislators.

The impact of GFO accountability systems on the NPA is paradoxical. On the one hand, managers perceive the GFO systems as a force for mediocrity; on the other hand, as a force for improvement. Sometimes, they perceive that GFO systems compel, and thereby enable, fundamental and meaningful changes. At other times, they perceive them to require superficial, meaningless, and burdensome ones.

One compliance coordinator, who worked for a GFO before accepting his current NPA position, confirms that GFO accountability systems can be a "powerful force for mediocrity" among NPAs.

> If the [GFO] says, "You must do A, B, and C," even if you're running a clinical program which you think meets the intent of doing A, B, and C, you're going to stop. You're going to make sure that you do A, B, and C exactly that way. If you don't do that, the first time you get the audit result back that tells you that you're out of compliance because you did A, B, and D, you'll change.
>
> So programs that were poor have a real incentive to get their act together, at least enough to meet those standards. Programs that were strong tend to divert their resources from whatever it was that was making them strong in the first place towards doing A, B, and C. It tends to create a good deal more homogeneity.

He says "the most important thing" a GFO must do when it contracts for a service is ensure that the service "meets a minimum acceptable level." But, he concludes, the "saddest and hardest dilemma" about the contracted services game is that "auditing is absolutely essential and that it will also have some counterproductive effects on strong organizations."

Although GFO accountability systems can be a force for mediocrity, they can also be a force for improvement, in both weak and strong NPAs and in the entire service delivery system. One way that GFOs operate as a force for improvement is by "grading on a curve," evaluating NPAs based on their performance relative to other NPAs'.

Managers' recognition of this grading system is reflected in their perception that all GFO standards are not equally important. They share diverse examples indicating this is how GFO accountability systems operate. As one explains, GFO regulations may far exceed the possibility for compliance. She says the requirements for services to the retarded are "two inches thick," and while compliance on "the key indicators" is essential, it would be "impossible" to have "no deficiencies."

Another indication that GFOs grade on a curve is that they may stop holding the NPA accountable for a standard no NPAs can meet. Several managers talk of their frustration with a GFO standard regarding staff turnover. One says that after her NPA fails on compliance with that standard, she refuses to write an improvement plan and tells the auditor, "I can't even address this issue; this is a citywide problem" related to low salaries and the regulatory burden. When the GFO sends her a list of things she should do to lower the turnover rate she tells them repeatedly, "We've already done those things." Finally, when she refuses to do or write more on the subject, the GFO monitor says, "All right, I'll just write down here that it's already been done." The manager notes:

> But now they're no longer rating turnover because it's such a horrendous problem. I'm sure there wasn't one agency that passed for staff turnover last year.

Sometimes GFOs grade on multiple curves. This is manifest in a realization that there are homogeneous standards for heterogeneous services for diverse population groups. Because her NPA is "dealing with the most emotionally disturbed children in the whole system," a compliance coordinator explains they never meet a major GFO requirement to discharge children from residential care in twenty-four months. Yet after each audit, the GFO requires an improvement plan regarding this requirement:

"And we'll tell them, 'This is ridiculous. When are you going to stop bugging us with this?'"

> They understand. Somehow, they haven't gotten around to making different requirements, different expectations, for different kinds of programs. Everybody gets treated the same. So we keep going through the motions, and we respond like everybody else does. The bottom line is that everything's not relevant to everybody equally, but yet that's basically how it's set up.

Although she continues "going through the motions," she knows the GFO does not care that her NPA is out of compliance on this requirement because "they would make it an issue" if it "really bothered them."

A compliance coordinator suggests that accrediting bodies can affect the curve of GFO accountability systems. When GFOs incorporate Joint Commission standards in their own regulations, "everybody's reading" is that the GFO will not seriously monitor compliance with those regulations "because they assume that if you can be accredited by Joint Commission for your quality-assurance program then you can damn well be accredited by [the GFO]."

This coordinator explains that Joint Commission raises a standard as soon as an organization meets the existing one and describes Joint Commission's "theory" of accountability: "We are going to keep the mechanical rabbit running in front of you in our never-ending quest to improve the quality of care." As an example, he says the facility with the "best quality-assurance program in New York State" was faulted this year "for not having done something that we will not even be able to think about doing here for three years." Joint Commission never mentions the issue when they audit the coordinator's NPA; "somehow" they "knew that we're not there yet."

So that it's a very strange process where it's never like you can be the best and therefore it's okay. There's always something more to achieve in a given area.

The GFO this manager once worked for also grades on the curve.

> The system as a whole was below the standard. So that to say we are going to give problems to all the agencies that are doing unsatisfactory work in this area would have been crazy. We would have been beating up on the whole system, and you would have frittered away all your energy. So instead, we picked up the bottom of the group.
> We couldn't grade on the curve publicly because the [GFO] was out there saying that this is unsatisfactory performance. So we branded everyone unsatisfactory, which created a great deal of resentment in the agencies, understandably so. "What do you mean? We're doing better than 75 percent of the people out there. How can we be unsatisfactory? Your standards are stupid." But, in fact, you could be unsatisfactory. We would never mention it to you. But some other agencies that were exactly at the left-hand end of the curve, we'd give them a real hard time. Well, next year when the curve shifts over to the right, somebody who was here last year is further along the curve, so now we're saying, "You guys have got to clean up your act in this area."

When NPAs receive their ratings, he explains they also, in effect, get the GFO's curve because they receive the system average on each audited variable for the current and preceding years.

GFO accountability systems can compel fundamental changes, both positive and negative, in the NPA. Sometimes GFOs force NPAs to change the client population they serve. One manager explains that the GFO, in effect, requires her NPA to expand its charter from serving children to the age of twenty-one to also serving retarded adults. The GFO brings this pressure when it is forced, by court order, to move these retarded adults from institutions into community facilities.

An executive director explains that a GFO initially wants to know which client population the NPA serves most effectively. It is acceptable for her to say they work best where drugs are not the presenting problem, with families with infants and young children. However, with substance abuse increasing and appropriate services insufficient, the GFO compels her NPA to train staff to serve clients with this problem.

A number of managers describe the GFO accountability system as forcing their NPA from what one calls "mush" to administrative structure. This manager describes what happens when the program she directs in a very large NPA goes from being foundation- to GFO-funded.

> If you want to get into the system, then you better know that you're going to give up something in order to get something.

She says, "The biggest change for us was losing our time," because prior to receiving the GFO funding:

> We were pretty much doing what we wanted to do. It was very creative. That's why we could do all this proposal writing. We didn't have requirements other than what the [NPA] had.

She also gives up "clinical freedom" because of regulations regarding how many visits must be made by which staff in what period of time.

The GFO funds the program because of its volunteers; but to meet GFO requirements, the NPA must change its emphasis from volunteer home visiting to professional case management.

The manager describes what this change is like for her, as she moves from being part of a "mushed family," a "team all on the same level," to being the program director:

> That we did it as long as we did and got the money we did speaks to other things, but it doesn't speak to a good structure of problem solving and who's in charge and boundary issues. The process was a real dilemma in going from that program to this program—my asserting and taking over responsibility of becoming the program manager. That was about a six- to twelve-month period of time where I had to go asserting myself, where I would have to help [a key volunteer] in being included in some meetings, but not in clinical meetings—where, in the old days, everything was all mushed together. To deal with her feelings and issues around boundaries being set up, structures being set up.

A compliance coordinator says he anticipates the implementation of a quality-assurance process in the NPA, because it asks staff to "pinpoint" and follow up on problems "more precisely," to transform the NPA's management effort from bureaucratic mush to a more productive structure.

> That is, instead of saying, "Okay, we've identified a need, we talked for an hour about how to address the need," and the discussion sort of peters away, which is something that happens in every bureaucracy—the goad is always there to say, "Oh, my God, wait a minute, this is part of quality assurance. We're going to have to say what it is that we're going to do about this. And we're going to have to look at it again in a month or two to see whether it worked, and maybe it won't work."

While she believes the "record keeping the city has forced us into doing" is much more complicated than her NPA would have used, an executive director says:

> I like it because it enables us to check on how much work
> people are doing, the number of hours they're putting
> down for certain services, and that they're allocating their
> time properly. It gives us a pretty good picture of the
> work of the agency.

While one executive director strongly criticizes the GFO's expenditure of funds on forced computerization, other managers are enthusiastically introducing computerization into their NPAs. Somewhere in between, an executive director purchases a computer primarily to cope with GFO reporting requirements, but says he is pleased that a benefit for him will be "more accurate knowledge."

> I don't care about unduplicated count by day, but it's
> really helped formalize the structure of keeping track of
> how many kids are coming through. Because you tend to
> depend on certain generalized knowledge that you have,
> and it may or may not be accurate.

A compliance coordinator explains that compared to other agencies, her NPA is "really ahead of the game" because twenty years before, the finance director "had foresight to know that people can't survive without computers with all the complications that keep getting added on to these systems." She explains that having the computer capability to comply with GFO financial accountability requirements makes it "natural" to extend that capability to other GFO requirements.

Her NPA's computerized compliance capability then generates internal pressure for computer use beyond GFO accountability from staff who "want something back [from computer use] for themselves." The coordinator, with the finance director, "who has been the motivator for a long time," some clinical staff, and researchers, in what again seems a "natural flow," get together "to get a little more sophisticated and go beyond compliance issues with the computer" by developing a "comprehensive child information system."

For another compliance coordinator, the major impact of GFO accountability systems on NPAs is a shift in focus from individual cases to aggregate data. This shift, he believes, will "turn" a quality-assurance instrument "into something that's actually helpful to the program directors, that really is influencing the program, as opposed to something that you can say on paper is influencing the program." He explains why having social workers "integrate these new tools" into their professional "tool kit" is going to be "very hard work."

> Like most professions, this is a profession which resists aggregation. It's very much focused on individual cases, and if you say to somebody, "What's happening in your clinic?" you will often get back a response that describes the two most interesting cases that the person has seen that day. If you try to talk in aggregates, people can always tell a good story about why you shouldn't be mushing all those cases together because every case does have a rich life of its own, and the nature of the jobs discover the richness of the case.
> So to say, "You served thirty-seven schizophrenic clients in that clinic last year. What happened to your schizophrenic group, as opposed to your mood disorder group?" people don't like talking in those terms. What quality assurance really is all about, and what I think a lot of contract monitoring is all about, is being able to aggregate things in a reasonable and useful way. Not because you want people to stop paying attention to the case, but because you learn a different set of things by talking about aggregates than you do by talking about individual cases.

This manager says his "task of the future" is to make "meaningful" instruments addressing aggregates and "to help people see them as meaningful and use them." He is finding that "the closer you get to things that are people's daily concerns, the easier it is." One area he believes will be helpful is the computerized analysis of incidents (e.g., fights, suicide attempts) in residential facilities for emotionally disturbed children.

> To be able to say to a clinic director, "Your incidents seem to be happening on Sundays, in the late afternoon, early evening, in a very disproportionate number," where the administrator will immediately make the connection, "That's when the kids are coming back from home visits, it's a very chaotic time on the weekend, maybe we need to do something to shore up the program then?" A place I hope to be able to get to, "In a given cottage, isn't it striking that 60 percent of the incidents involve the same staff member? Maybe that person needs to have some work done with him on how we respond to provocative behaviors from the kids?"

His efforts to have staff use aggregate data has, he believes, been helpful to the NPA's residential programs, but not the small, day programs.

> I think it's much easier in the residences because the kids are there twenty-four hours a day. So many different things are happening that you almost need to count them. But in our smaller programs it's particularly difficult, and I'm very sympathetic to how difficult it is. We have day-treatment programs with thirty kids in them where if you try to aggregate data on a universe of thirty, it's just not going to tell you a whole hell of a lot. These people get screwed both ways. Not only do they have the least useful data, but they also have the small staff. The work of collecting the data and looking at it is very hard work for them to do.

He then relates his assessment of the impact of his efforts on the senior administrative staff and what he expects will evolve as his focus on aggregate data intensifies.

I think that I've developed good relationships with them and that, at the moment, they primarily perceive it as helpful because they are, after all, in charge of making sure that the quality-assurance program is implemented in all of their programs. The more that I can make it easy to do that, work with their program directors, and spare them the burden of having to pay attention to this when they'd like to pay attention to a hundred other issues, the easier their jobs are. So, that's been the primary perception so far.

Now the more detailed we get, the more we will have a tension because, on the one hand, I will help them focus on the problems that they see in their own operation. On the other hand, I will make those problems more visible, and there'll be somebody outside of their control who's going to be asking questions about them and getting information and that will be threatening to them. That's all sort of personal relationships, a little bit of stroking, a little bit of saying, "Sorry, we've got to do it."

Another manifestation of the NPA's shift from mush to structure with the implementation of GFO accountability systems is a shift from clinical to administrative supervision. After having deficiencies cited in a GFO audit, a manager changes her supervisory approach.

I look at the monthly stats every month. I never gave the workers feedback on, "Oh, this client only had X contact on Y this month. What's going on? We need to talk about it." Now, I'm going to have to do that. That's now one of my ways of trying to improve our meeting standards. "If there's only one contact, have you considered a home visit and why not?"

Now when they give me the UCRs [uniform case records] to sign off as the supervisor before the monitor comes to read them, I ask them, "Are your home visit standards up, too?" Or, "Is this plan up to snuff? If not, let's talk about it, and I need to write a justification if it's legitimate." Is it just resistance on the part of the worker? What is it? Is it casework issues?

All different kinds of issues—all of which I should be doing anyway or I feel I should have been doing anyway, but there's a lot to do in a small program, and you have a staff of eight clinical people, you can't stay on top of everything all the time, and you don't. That's the way it is. But now, at least, this mechanism is in place, where I can at least plan to give them feedback every month on the ones that are short home visits or face-to-face visits.

For several managers, the contracted services game is played with paper. They view GFO accountability systems as compelling the NPA to shift from provision of service to provision of paperwork. A compliance coordinator illustrates the magnitude of the problem for social workers whom the GFO requires to track seventy-two variables for each child in foster care.

If you think of it on a grid, you're going up this crazy diagonal and trying to figure out where you are on that diagonal—whether you need to see the parents once a week, once every two weeks, once a month, once every three months, or once every six months, which are all possible depending on the discharge objective, the age of the child, and the length of time in care. It becomes very frustrating for the worker to try to keep track of it.

An executive director says that when his GFO home-care program went to performance-based contracting all of his staff quit within three months "because of the amount of paperwork." Another manager explains that "the whole accountability paperwork part of the job" has so exceeded provision of service that "for the little amount of money that child welfare agencies can pay, master's level social workers who are really interested in doing clinical work don't want to come here anymore and do this."

Some managers believe that GFOs compel NPAs to make only superficial changes. While not fundamental to NPA operations, these changes are often burdensome and time consuming. For one compliance coordinator, an impact of the GFO accountability system on his NPA is the necessity of translating the work the NPA is doing into GFO language. He explains the pervasiveness of the GFO requirement that all of the NPA's work under the contract be guided by "measurable, quantifiable goals." Then he delineates the equally pervasive NPA effort to make no changes in their work, but to make whatever changes are necessary to describe that work in terms of the GFO-required "behavior mod approach."

> We explain that whether or not that is the approach you are using with a child or the family, what they [the GFO] are looking for is things that they can monitor very quantitatively. Therefore, whatever you do, you're going to need to translate into that language when you write it down. That includes in your progress notes, in the UCR [uniform case record] and all the different places you need to.
> We keep avoiding as much as possible calling it behavior mod. We say that you have to take what you're doing and you've got to put it into a measurable means that can be monitored and that the change can be determined. It has to be something that isn't a theoretical or subjective interpretation. It has to be something that you can sit there, and A has moved to B. If you word everything in that way, then you can get away with it, as long as the B ends up being realistic.

He goes on to explain the "challenge" of teaching staff to make this translation.

It really depends on the individual. A lot of that's one-to-one. How do you do it? Some people sit there and they'll think of A to B and what they want to go from A to B. Then they can see A to B and then translate straight. Parallel translation. Sometimes we take a "what does A loo : like in a behavior sense? What behaviors are they doing right now? Let's go back to A. Where do you want them to be in six months? Now, what behaviors does that look like?" See, you're using individual links that way. Some people will see it that way where they'll take A, convert it. Go to B, then convert it. Others can just convert at the parallel lines. A to B is the same as A to B. So it really depends on how that individual thinks and works with behaviors, how comfortable they are with how they're going to go about making that translation. I'm more concerned that they're able to; whichever method they use is really up to them.

For another compliance coordinator, a deplorable impact of GFO accountability systems is the necessity of developing parallel systems. He explains that the GFO-required quality-assurance process "was really invented by [the GFO] for hospitals" and is "overlaid" on existing NPA supervisory processes.

Now, the basic characteristic of hospitals is that physicians have admitting privileges, and basically once they've qualified for admitting privileges, they don't have supervisors. You just put the patient in the hospital and take care of him and when the patient's ready, you discharge him. All of this is overlay: "Say, wait a minute, we want to make sure that the services we're providing are appropriate and we're only keeping people in the hospital for as long as they need to be here." There's an overlay to look at the work that people are doing.

In a mental health setting, that overlay already existed before quality assurance. Every clinician has a supervisor.

Every supervisor works for an office director. Every case has to be approved by a psychiatrist every six months. There are multiple layers of review involved in the normal work of the office and that's part of the reason why quality assurance can seem so burdensome to people. Because it is superimposed upon processes that already exist.

Although the creation of this parallel process theoretically requires superficial, not fundamental, changes in the NPA, he tries to get "around that" and make the change fundamental by focusing on aggregate data.

Managers exercise multiple-process and goal-oriented strategies for effecting change in GFO accountability systems. However, GFOs actually induce NPAs to influence GFO accountability systems.[3] For the NPA, a coalition of NPAs is vital in playing the game of contracted services. Evidently, GFOs also believe NPA coalitions are vital; they pay for them. As one executive director explains:

There's a whole group of agencies that provide rehab services, workshops. They have a statewide association, and they have a hired executive director and a staff in Albany to do their lobbying. We have a contract with them so that this same office and people are providing the same sorts of services for both. We're allowed to pay dues into [NPA coalition] out of our contract, so I think we paid about four hundred dollars last year. Statewide, the [coalition] budget is about fifty thousand dollars, and we pay this outfit [rehab coalition] thirty-one thousand dollars this year.

NPAs are able to influence the GFO accountability system through this coalition, funded by the GFO, of community residences for the mentally ill. This executive director gives an example of the exercise of that influence when the GFO, which wants more cooperation in discharge planning between state hospitals and community residences, tries to put in the contract a clause requiring NPAs to take 50 percent of their clients from state hospitals. When representatives of the NPA coalition and the GFO meet to discuss the proposed clause, he explains, "it was a little power struggle."

> They [GFO] did not want to be perceived as negotiating the contract with us. We're an "advisory group to advise them, to help them to set policy, but not to negotiate." I don't think I would have said that if I were them, but they said it.

Despite the GFO's insistence that it will not negotiate with the NPA coalition, it appears to do just that.

> The meeting only lasted about an hour. At one point we broke and caucused separately and came back into the room. They made the offer that they would take out the original wording of the 50 percent and put in this benign kind of clause in the principles section that would refer to the intent to take referrals from state facilities and reference an agreement that would be worked out and attached to the contract.

The executive director believes the GFO agreed to take the 50 percent requirement out of the contract

> because what began surfacing—I think this was the strongest piece—was that there're so many circumstances that come up around the state about what is an inpatient, for instance. Somebody who's been out of the hospital one day, and you take him into the program? Do you get credit for that as a state person? Some agencies take a lot of people who aren't state people but who would be state

people if they hadn't been diverted to a particular community mental health center. That was the case in one
agency upstate. So, we wanted to allow for that. So this
agreement could allow for individual circumstances. I
think that was the most forceful thing. The [GFO] goal
really was to have the agreement [between the state hospitals and community residences] put in place.

Despite the GFO's capitulation, they refused to show the coalition the wording before sending it out to individual NPAs because "they felt that was stepping over what our recognized role
was in this process."

We said we were in a very awkward position. We're the
leadership of an organization that's being asked to offer
advice back to the membership, and we can't do that.
They said, "Well, looks like you don't trust us. We're telling you what we're going to put in there. And if it's not
as we say it is then you can certainly alert us once you
have the contract."
We said, "Look, they're going to get this thing, and
they're going to start calling us to find out what to do."
We didn't say specifically we were going to tell people not
to sign the contracts, but that's what we're going to do because we have an attorney in Albany who will review the
thing for us. It's a legal question.

GFOs also enable NPAs to influence GFO accountability systems by using NPA managers to coach other NPA managers. One
manager describes how he is "borrowed by the city" to help train
NPAs.

They'll call [the executive director] and say, "Look, can
_____ come down to a meeting on this date for the
day? We're doing a meeting for voluntary agencies on in-
quiries on the system, and we know that he does a lot of it
from your end, and we'd like him to be able to assist us."

Another manager explains there is an NPA coalition effort to have the GFO cut down on its monitoring and provide more technical assistance. Lacking this capability, the GFO uses her to train NPAs because, "I have been around so long and know so much." GFO staff advise NPAs with new contracts.

> "Why don't you call up _____ and see how they do it at [her NPA] because their system is working." Which I'm glad to do except that if I get too many of those calls, that's just not appropriate. When they expanded at one point, when there were a lot of new contracts out, I was getting a lot of those kinds of calls, and again I didn't mind doing it, but it just didn't seem an appropriate situation. I could also be telling somebody a lot of wrong information.

This same manager is asked by the GFO to coach a new auditor.

> I was told that she had been assigned to me because she was new, and the expectation was that I could help her learn the job.

In some instances, GFOs require coaching assistance from NPAs by the way they structure accountability systems. Several managers explain that they "waste so much time" because the GFO, which contracts out for fiscal auditors, sends different ones as often as every year, and the NPAs then have "to train them from scratch." An executive director explains:

> Every year we've had a different auditor. That's a terrible problem. Just when somebody gets to know you and how you're set up, they're reassigned. We're complicated. We're small, but we're complicated. We have seven bank accounts. There're always things that intersect and overlap. Every year we have to break in a new auditor for the city.

Perhaps the most subtle influence NPAs have on GFO accountability systems is through their own staff, whom GFOs hire. Some NPA staff work "at the base standards in pay" because NPAs do not have non-GFO funds to supplement salaries. GFO salaries are often "considerably more" than NPAs'. A manager describes how the GFO routinely "bought out" his NPA's staff.

> We have been dubbed as one of the best training facilities in the city system, and the city comes looking through our staff and hires out from under us. I'd say somewhere between five and ten people a year get bought out by the city.

He concludes:

> It's, in a sense, a joke, but it's also very sad in that we've been dubbed one of the better [GFO] training centers and that one of our biggest problems is staff turnover.

NOTES

1. See Harold H. Weissman, "Accreditation, Credentialing, and Accountability," *Administration in Social Work*, Winter 1981, pp. 41–42.
2. Recent research emphasizes the inadequacy of public administration theory to address the GFO/NPA relationship in contracting and other GFO tools creating third-party government. "To come to terms with these new forms of public action, therefore, new theories and concepts will be needed. Instead of command and control, such theories will have to emphasize *bargaining* and *persuasion*. Instead of the clarification of directives, they will have to stress the manipulation of *incentives*." Lester M. Salamon, ed., assisted by Michael S. Lund, *Beyond Privatization: The Tools of Government Action* (Washington, D.C.: The Urban Institute, 1989), p. 13.
3. This phenomenon of GFOs' inducing NPAs' influence appears to be an interesting variation of the "capture theory," subsumed in the

political-economy model of government regulation. See Robert H. Miles and Arvind Bhambri, *The Regulatory Executives* (Beverly Hills, Calif.: Sage Publications, 1983), pp. 17–20; and Barry M. Mitnick, *The Political Economy of Regulation: Creating, Designing, and Removing Regulatory Forms* (New York: Columbia University Press, 1980), pp. 206–14.

CHAPTER   EIGHT

SERVICE DELIVERY

The contracted services game is not one game; it is at least two disguised as one, as if one team came onto the field to play baseball and the other to play football.

> In the absence of a firm theoretical basis for government-nonprofit relations, neither government officials nor non-profits have managed to develop a meaningful and co-herent set of standards in terms of which to guide their interactions. Rather, both sides have tended to view the relationship from their own perspective and to apply standards that are rigid and absolute.[1]

To play this rather bizarre amalgam of a game, managers must perpetually accommodate the different perspective and standards of GFOs while they affirm their NPAs' perspective and standards. This ongoing, messy process of accommodation and affirmation has many manifestations and raises innumerable questions about the service delivery system.

Which Characteristics of the NPA Are Significant?

Many managers talk about the significance of the size of their NPAs.[2] Several, in agencies of varying sizes, feel that because their NPAs are smaller than GFOs, they can deliver quality services "in a way that's impossible for the city." Simply put, NPA administrative staff know more of the clients and staff; clients know more of the staff. As one manager says:

> I think because any voluntary agency, even the big voluntary agencies, are smaller than the city [GFO], we're able to concern ourselves with quality in a way that's impossible for the city. Because there aren't any really hard and fast, observable measures of quality. It's just not that concrete.
>
> The percentage of cases served by the city that [the GFO commissioner] can know about is tiny. The percentage of cases that [our NPA executive director] can know about is not as small. She can tell the board about a bigger percentage of actual families getting service. She and I can know about a bigger percentage of clients who are doing well and benefiting from the service and clients who are not benefiting. The line workers are the key to the whole thing. [The executive director] and I know all of the one hundred employees so if they're doing a good job or if they're screwing up, we know about it. If you work with the city, there's no way.

A manager for another NPA talks about the virtues of an NPA's having a range of services and the difficulty of adequate communication, even when the NPA is relatively small.

[This NPA's] really medium-sized for agencies in New York. What's terrific is the range that we do, but that also makes it more difficult. Also more exciting. I think, much richer for the people who work here. You're working with a problem family: You can plug somebody into a literacy program; you can get a mother into a displaced-home-maker program. You've got a teen parent program; you've got schools. You've just got such a range of services at your beck and call. Although when we're all so busy, even at this fairly small place, we don't do as good a job as we should keeping people informed about everything that's going on.

A manager in a large NPA believes that being larger enables the agency to have people with "pretty good smarts" and to have "the machinery already in place" to handle all the fiscal issues with contracting. However, she still does her budget because it keeps her "very in tune."

A program director feels that the size of a contracted service in relationship to other services in an NPA is also significant. Although other, much larger NPAs, with presumably more leverage than hers have the same contract, this service represents "maybe 2 percent of their program," while it represents "20 percent" of her NPA's. Therefore, these larger NPAs "can't put the bulk of their time and effort," for themselves and the smaller NPAs, into "making a big noise" regarding major problems with this contracted service.

For several managers, the relative continuity of NPA, as opposed to GFO, management is another significant characteristic of the NPA. Continuity, for managers, encompasses both leadership stability and an enduring NPA service philosophy. One compliance coordinator says her NPA "developed an identity over time," despite being almost 100 percent funded by GFOs. That identity she equates with the NPA's philosophy, reflected in the management staff: "People who go for quality first and will always choose the human side over the piece of paper."

An executive director reports that over a five-year period all the directors in an NPA coalition stayed in their positions while all but one of the GFO incumbents changed, most repeatedly.

> We've been around a lot longer than the state has. We're constantly telling them what happened. Remember the '83 incident? "No, we weren't there." The commissioner wasn't there. His assistants weren't there. This Bureau of Residential Services guy wasn't there. His supervisor is a new position; he's only been there three months. So of this group we were talking to, the budget director was the only guy that was there.
>
> The lower-line people were there, but the decision makers weren't. They move around a lot from one state agency to another and from one state to another. The mortality rate is high, and the commissioner is on his way out. He's under siege now and he's going to be gone. There'll be a lot of changeover then. A new guy brings in his people.

In addition to their size and continuity, managers say NPAs, even if they are 100-percent GFO-funded, are characterized by greater control than GFOs.[3] Describing this sense of control, one manager says NPAs "minimize" having "regulations about how we're supposed to do everything."

> In general, I would think that people would work here and want to be in a private agency rather than government because there's a sense of more control over what they do and how they do it and input into that. Because

they do have more. Because I think in a government, if this were simply a field office of [a GFO], we would be loaded down with all kinds of regulations about how we're supposed to do everything, and we really try to minimize that. I think that we're able to.

Another explains why being an NPA, despite 80-percent GFO funding, "makes a big difference."

We have more autonomy because we contract with several different government agencies, and we do make decisions that the city can't make. We decide to stop providing a service because we decided that was not the best use of our effort at that time. We decide not to serve certain clients because they're not appropriate for our program. We decide to have different standards than the city.

Managers' efforts to affirm the perspective and standards of their NPAs while accommodating those of the GFO are perhaps clearest in their diverse efforts to maintain control in their daily work. Because she believes it is critical to preserve "the professionalization of the service," one manager engages in a "constant struggle" to have NPA staff perceive her totally GFO-funded program "as very separate" from the GFO. She insists the program not be called by the GFO's name, does not use the GFO's name on business cards, and is "making sure" the "focus" of the program is maintained and it is seen as "a very active part" of the NPA.

Another manager's ongoing efforts to maintain control are reflected in her struggle to have contracted programs evolve from client needs rather than from GFO requirements. A GFO's request for proposals for dropout prevention programs encourages services to be based on needs assessment. However, when the contracts are written, the GFO insists that six services be offered in all programs "for a thousand dollars a kid." She tells the GFO that this is impossible and that "they distort the development of these programs by requiring that we do all things simultaneously."

> If we had been able to go in there and sit down with the principal, look at the kids, get to know the kids, and see what was needed, we would have organically developed a program with the right kind of mix, based upon needs and school-driven. This was an imposition of a structure from the top. It forced us to spend a lot of time and energy on services that (a) we're not as good at delivering and (b) are not necessarily top-priority services in terms of keeping kids in school but which were required in the contract, so we had to do it.

She says that "over the last couple of years," she and other NPAs have successfully "argued" with the GFO: "If you can't drop those components, allow us to introduce wording which gives us latitude and flexibility."

For one executive director, the struggle to affirm his NPA's perspective and standards translates to competing for GFO funds. Because his coalition's programs represent only forty or fifty million dollars of a GFO budget of over a billion dollars and there is such rapid turnover in GFO management for those programs, he says NPAs learn "we've really got to take care of ourselves." How to do so they discover "from other agencies that have been at it longer." The NPAs also realize when they compete with other state agencies for inclusion in the governor's budget, "We can't depend on [our GFO] to be our defenders; they've learned a lot, but we still know more."

Another executive director sees the effort to get GFO funding as part of the struggle for control. She explains that her NPA seeks GFO funding, not only because it is secure, but "to try to have some influence, some impact, even if it were minimal, on the system, because the families we work with are caught up in it."

Does the GFO or the NPA "Own" the Client?

When the GFO contracts with the NPA to provide a service, is the NPA serving GFO clients or do those clients, by virtue of the contractual relationship, become NPA clients? This question appears to have profound implications. Philosophically and practically, if the NPA is the GFO's agent serving GFO clients, the NPA's commitment to the primacy of the client's interest becomes ambiguous.

The NPA identifies clients according to GFO criteria in some contracted services. In others, the GFO sends clients to the NPA. Regardless of how clients get to the NPA, for several managers the most troubling manifestation of the question of client ownership is confidentiality. From whom is the client protected against violations of his or her privacy?

One manager captures the "bottom line" of the difference in the GFO and NPA perceptions of clients.

> The problem is that [the GFO] and the state, very clearly, see our patients as their patients. We would like to maintain a sense that they are [the NPA's]. Bottom line, the reality is the state and the city see them as their patients, and we're a contracted agency to service their patients.

This "reality," she explains, "came out most clear" to her when an NPA coalition group met with the GFO about a new requirement that NPAs transmit patient identifiable information to the GFO for input into its new computer system. When the NPAs express concern about access to the data, the response is

> "state and [GFO] people do [have access], but this is not going outside of the system. These are our patients, so we're really not breaking confidentiality issues."

The manager says the NPAs' response to this GFO assertion about client ownership and confidentiality is rage. The GFO says it needs the information "to track patients through the system"; NPAs say data that is not client-identifiable should suffice. NPAs believe an agreement regarding confidentiality, resulting from their lawsuit when contracted preventive services began, was to continue with computerization. With protest letters prepared by the coalition, NPAs submit the requested information, but because of the current political climate, lawyers advise them further legal action could lead to less confidentiality protection.

An executive director says she is seeing her "worst fears come true" as the GFO computerizes and uses client information collected in one program to recruit for other GFO-funded programs: "Families' privacy is being violated in just the way that we were afraid it would be." As an example, she explains that one of her staff hears at a GFO advisory council meeting that a GFO pilot program to serve pregnant and parenting teenagers has

> gotten their caseload up nicely because [GFO] Information Systems was letting them have from their computer the name of any family where a seventeen-year-old or sixteen-year-old had a baby. They were sending them a letter, and they were going to the house.

Soon thereafter, another NPA staff person reports that a sixteen-year-old mother with whom she is "just starting to get this kid where she might come" for services has told her never to return to the house. The young woman has "thrown out" workers from other agencies before, saying she does not want to see anyone else. This time, her rejection is precipitated by a visit from a representative of the GFO pilot program. The executive director learns, "Sure enough, the [GFO] computer had coughed up that kid." When the NPA asks a GFO staff person "what's going on," the response is defensive and angry.

> "We have a right to anything that's in that [computer]
> because we're all paid by [the GFO] so we should have
> a right to see anything that's on their record. We're
> all being paid by the same system. We're working for
> them."

The executive director laments, "I have a lot of questions about
that."

Another NPA manager is unequivocal: "Our advocacy position and our service position is that they are our clients." Managers' perception of clients is influenced, too, by how they
believe clients see themselves and, perhaps, how they encourage clients to see themselves. An executive director explains that
from the point of view of families, her NPA's services are available, free, to them all. When the GFO contract begins, the NPA
"moved families right into that."

> As far as families were concerned, there was no differ-
> ence, except they had to sign a 2921. That takes a little
> time sometimes. And sometimes you'll work with a fam-
> ily for months before they sign it.

Another manager says that because clients see themselves as
the NPA's clients, "they might indeed be very wary about what
they would share or whether they'd accept the service at all" if
the NPA is going "to pass" information to the GFO. An executive
director says her recent experience

> justifies the fears of so many families who say once
> you're poor and you're in that computer, your life is an
> open book to any public employee who wants to poke
> around.

Another manager describes as the "sad part" that:

Most of our clients are on public assistance, and they're so used to making their lives an open book that they really are not as upset about confidentiality as we are.

A compliance coordinator concurs that "patients have less reaction to it than we do." But she believes this is "partially" true because:

We don't want to fully educate the client to all the ramifications of all these things, because we really see the needs that these clients have and want to work with them.

Thus, she concludes, this issue of affirming the client's right to privacy is "a very difficult, tricky area."

What Is the Function of the NPA Board of Directors?

The ultimate authority for an NPA is its board of directors. The limited empirical research indicates, however, that boards' exercise of this authority is typically reactive to staff initiative, internally conflict-aversive, and interactive with the executive director.[4] The scope of research on the impact of government funding on the function of the NPA board or on the impact of the NPA board on government funding appears to be one study.[5]

This study, a survey of NPAs in metropolitan New York City, found that "on the whole, Board Members appear to have but a perfunctory relationship to the influx of government funds to their agencies." The authors conclude that "the insufficient involvement of agency Boards in determining policy relating to the initiation and execution of government contracts" is a " 'danger point'" for NPAs, and they make suggestions for greater board involvement.[6]

Many managers seem to view the board as irrelevant in terms of the major political issues regarding contracted services. While some intimate a well-connected board president or director might be able to smooth the contracting process or even affect the awarding of a contract, these efforts generally appear to be narrow and specific and do not address universal problems. For many issues, the political forces appear too powerful and complex for a single director or board of directors to impact. When a major issue arises around the philosophy and planned implementation of a GFO program for home care for the elderly, for example, an executive director calls a special board meeting, the first in "fifteen or sixteen years." The board "got very upset" and has a meeting with city, state, and congressional representatives. Although "most of them were on our side," she says, "It didn't do any good." Why? "The governor wanted it. It was the governor's bill."

Several managers describe the board's involvement in contracting issues as limited to occasional letter writing or contact with political leaders about, for example, salary levels. Generally, managers do not believe it is appropriate or possible for the board to be involved in "operational issues." One manager says her board "does not get involved" in the struggle with the GFO about contract rates: "That doesn't seem like a board responsibility, especially not in an agency like this, which has so many programs." After explaining extensive efforts he makes through an NPA coalition to influence GFO's contracting for community residences for the mentally ill, an executive director says "there's really no need" for his board to get involved.

While managers view NPA coalitions as more significant and effective than boards in addressing the political issues of contracting, several view their boards as critical in financing the NPA's fundamental ability to affirm its perspective and standards. One manager says her directors, members of a religious order, keep the NPA solvent by making interest-free loans of hundreds of thousands of dollars to cover GFO payment delays lasting as long as several years. For other managers, the board finances the NPA's ability to affirm its perspective and standards in a much broader sense than solvency. In these NPAs, the board commits to keeping government funding under 50 percent of the NPA's budget "to maintain some kind of balance and control."[7] However, one manager notes "it's getting harder and harder" to raise the necessary philanthropic dollars to honor this commitment.

For managers for whom government funding is significantly more than 49 percent of the NPA's budget, sometimes as high as 95 percent, the board's fund raising is still perceived as pivotal. An executive director says her NPA has "kept our financial independence as much as we could by putting a lot of our own money into it." In a contracted program funded by a GFO for $116,000, her NPA will spend an additional $59,000. As a result, "we haven't only been able to give the little raises that the city ekes out."

Another executive director, whose GFO funding is over 95 percent of his NPA's budget, explains how he takes a nonfunctioning board and re-creates and mobilizes it to fund the capacity to supplement and develop existing and new GFO-funded programs.

> The board hadn't met in two years when I came, so that
> was the first problem. It's very important—the board's
> critical, and they've got to be your friends and you've got
> to be their friend. We use them a lot for advice if we want
> to do this or that or "What do you think?"—the event
> planning and pulling those things off. We need the
> money in order to develop new stuff. We're trying to get a
> school over here that would be to house all our staff and
> this education program; that's going to require about a

million bucks of renovation. [For another project] we've got a gap of about $280,000. Through our board, we've lined up somebody who will put that money up so we can start construction, but who we'll then pay back through fund-raising activities. Mostly, the new people I've brought on are in the real estate industry because I feel that there's a connection between what we're doing and housing and real estate.

What Are the Implications of NPA Subsidy of Contracted Services?

While managers value having other than GFO funds in their struggle to affirm the NPA perspective and standards, this value is somewhat tainted. Managers gain flexibility and control in having (or not having) NPA funds subsidize contracted services (or, less commonly, in having contracted services subsidize NPA programs) but participate in an inequitable service delivery system. Ralph Kramer reviews the relationship between NPAs and GFOs and concludes, "a focus on governmental versus voluntary versus profit-making auspices deflects attention from the major policy question of equity: *who* should get *what* services (Kamerman 1983)?"[8] Programs contracted by GFOs for the same service are not equal. The NPA subsidy of contracted services alters the value of the GFO dollar because the subsidy influences both who gets services and, more obviously, what level of services they get.

To the extent that the availability of an NPA subsidy influences which NPAs, each with accessibility to different populations, participate in which contracted services, the subsidy presumably alters who gets services. Summarizing her NPA's position with GFOs, a manager in a very large NPA is explicit about the significance of her NPA's ability to subsidize services.

"You're not going to tell us who we're going to serve. We're going to do it our way. And we have enough of an endowment so we can absorb the cost." That is a very important concept about this agency. This agency differs from every other agency in the city because of its endowment and because we literally get so much money in as bequests and donations [that] if we piss away a million, we'll get a million in.

I don't fill out contract applications unless it's a very specialized project, for under one hundred thousand to two hundred thousand dollars. I'm not interested. Because what it costs in overhead here and what it costs to set up a program, it's not worth it. It has to be something that's worth it, a major contract. Special research things I do.

They just put out an RFP, which wants the agencies to serve a terribly high-risk population, adolescents with AIDS, PINS [persons in need of supervision] kids, and some other mishmash. [This NPA] won't touch that. Forget it. It's not worth it to us because of the cost of care and how we provide it. It would be another major deficit program. We run [other programs] at a large deficit because of what we put in.

After talking about the necessity for NPA subsidies to alleviate GFO payment delays, another manager decries the implications for small, community-based NPAs.

It is highway robbery. I don't know if anybody else is paying any attention, but the reality is that it has gotten so complicated to contract that you have to be a certain size to be able to do it. So the notion of community-based stuff—relative to what we used to talk about in the '60s— forget it. It's dead.

Alteration of who is served is individual and specific when NPA subsidies enable a client to continue to be served when he or she is no longer eligible for GFO contracted services. A program director explains her NPA's subsidy means a high school senior, whom the GFO will not fund for his last six months in the NPA's contracted alternative-school program because he is over eighteen, can continue and graduate. An executive director describes what her NPA's subsidy means for whether clients are served.

> If we are going to continue seeing families beyond what is reimbursable or a nurse is going to spend three hours instead of the two hours that will be reimbursable, we'll pick it up. We'll fund-raise. So, you don't say to a patient, "Well, we're so sorry. We can't go on visiting you because your Medicare eligibility has expired." Or, "This service isn't strictly covered."

Other evidence that NPA subsidies alter who is served is the effort by GFOs to, in effect, seize the subsidies by making NPA "private matches" part of contract budgets or creating NPAs that solicit philanthropic contributions. An executive director says GFOs use these seizures to justify continued program funding to legislatures: "Look, the agencies are putting so much of their money in." When seizures enable GFOs to maintain or increase their funding of contracted services, the alteration can be in the direction of broader availability of services, and the "who is served" is presumably more equitable. However, the alteration may simultaneously be less equitable by limiting programs to those with access to NPAs with subsidies available for GFO seizure.

Because seizure restricts NPA flexibility and control, managers are vigorous in their efforts to limit the extent to which NPA funds are included in the contract amount. An executive director explains, "It's your money, but you're going to be just as accountable for it to the city as their money." Therefore, although it costs her NPA an additional fifty thousand dollars to provide a contracted service, she reduces the private share commitment to twenty thousand. Excluding the additional money from the private share has never become an issue with the GFO; she says, "And God help me if it does. I'll take the whole thing out." Another manager does not reveal her NPA's subsidy in the contract budget because, "I don't want to get on the hook of showing a private share, because then I'm on the hook forever."

An executive director conceptualizes one contracted service as an effort by the GFO to seize NPA subsidies and, in essence, NPAs, by "coopting" them. She then denounces the GFO practice of creating its own NPAs, thereby competing with NPAs for voluntary contributions.

> In government agencies, they're not supposed to compete for private funds with voluntary agencies, and they are doing it constantly. [A certain] city program is all private money. It's run by the [GFO], but it's all private money. There are ways to do it. You [the GFO] set up a separate corporation, you give them office space, and you help them go out and get private money. They set it up as a nonprofit corporation because they wanted to give the service, and there was no government money. But this way they have direct control of it, or indirect control of it. It's supposed to be a separate board and everything else, but the relationship is very close.

When the NPA subsidizes GFO contracts, the alteration that occurs in *who* receives services is sometimes subtle. The alteration in *what* services are received is often blatant. Managers give multiple examples of the difference having or not having an NPA subsidy makes in what clients, served under theoretically the same GFO contracts, receive. A manager, itemizing all the additional services available through her NPA's large subsidy, says clients are "basically fortunate to be in our care." She notes that "money speaks," and this ability to subsidize also gives her leverage to force the GFO to allow her NPA to reduce their contracted level of service commitment, thereby spending more per unit of service than the same GFO program in other NPAs.

For a manager in a "fairly small" NPA, the contracted services system is a "catch-22" in which NPAs with negligible ability to subsidize "get caught." The GFO's per diem reimbursement rate is based on each NPA's expenses two years before the current contract year. Lacking money "to lay out for things that we can worry about getting paid back for in a couple of years," her NPA can spend less on services than agencies with such money; therefore, the GFO gives them a lower per diem rate.

The executive director of another small NPA says that by doing "a lot of fund raising," her agency has been able to "do the work the way we felt it had to be done." They have also been able to subsidize, by more than 10 percent, contracted salaries.[9] As a result of this programmatic independence and "proper" pay, they have not "had the fast turnover that has plagued most of the agencies," and clients receive more consistent services.

NPA subsidy of contracted programs can also mean substantial differences in the degree to which staff time is consumed in administrative problems, rather than service provision. The manager in a large agency says she is "very lucky" because her NPA covers administrative supply costs exceeding the contract budget. Another manager describes her previous experience working for an NPA with no funds for subsidy.

> You lived by your contract, and you spent in accord.
> There were no frills. In other words, if the Xerox machine broke and there was no money, forget it. Pads of paper became a problem.

Should GFO Treatment of NPAs and FPOs Be the Same?

Managers grapple with yet another complex question about the role of NPAs in GFO service delivery. In recent years, there has been enormous growth in GFOs' contracting with FPOs [for-profit organizations] for human services, with little empirical research of the process or results.[10] Although managers talk about businesses in general, and not specifically about FPOs' providing services, their perceptions of the assumptions GFOs make in contracting with NPAs versus FPOs are significant.

To play effectively a game in which NPAs will increasingly have to compete with FPOs as well as other NPAs, social work administrators will need to become knowledgeable about similarities and differences between NPAs and FPOs.[11] They will need to acknowledge their preconceptions about NPAs and FPOs and subject them to rigorous testing. The complexity of this acknowledgement and testing of preconceptions is apparent from managers' contradictory perceptions: that GFO treatment of NPAs and FPOs is not the same, but should be and, paradoxically, that it is the same, but should not be.

One manager denounces what she perceives as the GFOs' treatment of NPAs as "quasi-public, attached at the hip," rather than "separate and distinct." She says GFOs seem to feel "you need them more than they need you" and expect NPAs to "take everything" in regard to the contract. Her NPA coalition seeks a "business relationship, not a lopsided relationship" with the GFO.

> I think we should be seen more as a business paid to do a job. I don't own you because I'm paying you to do something. It's always true in business that I pay you and expect something in return. [The GFO] wants to never let us get involved in any dialogue regarding the body of the contract and then presents it to us in two days and says, "Sign," with fifty million changes from last year. Is this the way business works? No negotiation?

Explaining that he and his NPA coalition colleagues have determined they must "read everything" in contracts "much more seriously now," an executive director is resentful that GFOs expect NPAs to trust their word about the interpretation of contractual requirements. He says their word clearly cannot be trusted, in part because those asking for trust often leave the GFO before the need for interpretation occurs. He perceives GFOs would never expect the same kind of trust from business.

In addition to believing that GFOs do not and would not treat businesses as they treat NPAs, other managers suggest businesspeople would not tolerate such GFO treatment. After explaining that she receives no money the first six months of each contract year and, therefore, cannot purchase program supplies during that period, a manager observes, "If a businessman came in and tried to run this program," he would be incredulous, go crazy, and be unable to function.

An executive director is indignant that GFOs assume NPAs have to be "forced" to "manage like a business," rather than allowing them to manage like a business.

> Let's say I'm a for-profit company and you're the city, and I contract with you to give you a product. The bottom line—it says I'm going to give you that product for a million and a half dollars. All you're interested in is that at the end of the year, you've got that product, and I haven't billed you more than a million and a half. You don't tell me how much I can pay my workers. You don't tell me what hours they have to work, where they have to work, when they have to work, how they have to work.
>
> But sometimes in nonprofit, the city takes that leeway and says to me, "Okay, I'm giving you a million and a half. You're going to have to provide X number of services. Along the way, I'm going to dictate to you who you can hire, the qualifications of your staff, how much you can pay them, what hours they can work, and everything else along the way." That's absurd. It's discrimination against the nonprofits because the assumption is that we don't know how to manage, that we're just a bunch of so-

cial workers, and we don't know about management. We don't know how to manage like a business, and they're going to force us into it. So instead, what they do is they force us to operate in gray areas so that we can give them that service at the end of the year for a million and a half.

Some managers, some of the time, believe that GFOs' treatment of NPAs and FPOs is not the same, but should be. At other times, however, they and other managers believe the opposite, that GFO treatment of NPAs and FPOs is the same but should not be. An executive director has a large performance-based contract, with unit rates set for each type of service. He decries the effect of GFOs' treating NPAs that are providing human services like FPOs that are "manufacturing widgets."

> We're not on an assembly line, manufacturing widgets, where you do ten thousand widgets and every widget is exactly the same and, unless you're a defense contractor, it's going to cost you three dollars.
> Every hour of counseling, every unit of counseling, is not the same. It's not going to cost you the same. One unit of counseling might be three hours. One unit of information—information is not calling up and saying, "Oh, I'm sorry, we don't do that, but call this number"— sometimes, a referral takes longer than a counseling session. If you spend two hours referring a person, it's one unit. If you spend two seconds—giving that person the phone number and saying, "Good luck"—it's the same unit. So what are you going to do? You're going to try to cut it short.

Another executive director says he has serious cash-flow problems because GFOs "treat us as a vendor," paying for the service long after it has been delivered. He bemoans the absurdity of the GFO's treating NPAs "just like they would a pencil company."

Several managers express concern about what they perceive as a GFO push to have human services managed by "people who are more business-minded." One says if her NPA were turned over to businesspeople "who don't know program," the agency would just "be meeting contractual requirements." Because "that's not what this agency's about," she says all the current staff would resign.

An executive director relates another manifestation of the offensive effort to "train us to be business managers." He describes his recent, frustrating experience as a student in a university program in administration of nonprofit organizations.

> None of the people who were [doing the] training were social workers, and none of them had ever been involved in managing a social service agency. The closest they had come to it was [a large hospital], which is to a social service agency like General Motors is to the guy that fixes my car. As a social worker, I resent that.
>
> When we talked about managing endowment funds, the example they used was for five million dollars. I looked around the room, and I said, "Does anybody here have a five million dollar endowment?" No. "So, don't talk to me about balancing my portfolio and these stocks and these municipals and these funds, because I'm not interested in that. I want to know what's the best two- or three-thousand-dollar CD [certificate of deposit] I can buy and how to do that." They couldn't do that.
>
> They talked about learning to say no. If you're at your desk, and you're doing paperwork, and somebody comes to you with problems—they're assuming that their problem is more important than what you're doing, and you have to be able to say no to that. I raised my hand, and I said, "Have you ever had an office that was a storefront, and some little old lady comes up to you while you're doing paperwork and tells you that she's about to be thrown out of her apartment?" No, they've never dealt with a client.

NOTES

1. Lester M. Salamon, "Partners in Public Service: The Scope and Theory of Government–Nonprofit Relations," in Walter W. Powell, ed., *The Nonprofit Sector: A Research Handbook* (New Haven, Conn.: Yale University Press, 1987), p. 113.
2. For a summary of the issues related to the size and structure of NPAs versus GFOs, see Ralph M. Kramer, "Voluntary Agencies and the Personal Social Services," in Powell, *The Nonprofit Sector*, pp. 243–44.
3. For a discussion of the "ideal human service bureaucracy," see Margaret L. Rhodes, *Ethical Dilemmas in Social Work Practice* (Boston: Routledge and Kegan Paul, 1986), pp. 139–44. To the extent that there is a difference in the degree to which clients "feel empowered, treated with dignity and respect, and cared for" in services delivered through NPAs as opposed to GFOs, perhaps the difference is due to this element of managerial control.
4. Melissa Middleton, "Nonprofit Boards of Directors: Beyond the Governance Function," and Kramer, "Voluntary Agencies," in Powell, *The Nonprofit Sector*, pp. 152–53, 244–46.
5. Related, sparse work focuses on the impact of NPAs on government. For example, a few studies determined that, contrary to the "mystique," NPA service innovations are rarely adopted by GFOs. Kramer, "Voluntary Agencies," in Powell, *The Nonprofit Sector*, pp. 248–52.
6. Nelly Hartogs and Joseph Weber, *Impact of Government Funding on the Management of Voluntary Agencies* (New York: Greater New York Fund/United Way, 1978), pp. 21–22, iii–iv. They conclude, "Conceivably, they [board members] do not consider the funded components as an integral part of the agency program, due to a possible conflict between their deep commitment to voluntarism and their perception of *having to accept government 'support'* as a negative development." The researchers make the following "suggestion" for boards.

   - active participation and involvement would serve the cause of voluntarism far better than the present aloof stance;
   - a closer identification with the corporate status of the agency and a more business-like self-perception might lead the Board to take the position that, as the "sellers" of a commodity (needed and specialized services) for which there is a "willing buyer"

(the government), they are entitled at the least to maximum payment, i.e. full recovery of costs; hence, they should be involved in contract negotiations and use their knowledge of "business" to adapt to the fiscal overview of the agency budget;
- because of Board Members' social standing and contacts, they could well be the most important and influential conduits to relate to government, serving both as interpreters and advocates on a policy level, towards improving sorely missing avenues of communication between the funding sources and the recipients;
- the pursuit of government funds is not significantly different from raising voluntary dollars, since the time when contributions and donations emanated only from the Board Members themselves and their peers is well in the past;
- if there is any doubt in Board Members' minds that these are proper functions for them, they need only to remind themselves that they are the policymakers and the fund raisers and that, last but not least, they are also legally responsible for the agency. (Pp. 21–22)

7. It is not clear, however, what the respective roles of board and staff are in generating nongovernment funding.
8. Sheila B. Kamerman, "The New Mixed Economy of Welfare: Public and Private," *Social Work* 28 (1983): 5–11, cited in Ralph M. Kramer, "Voluntary Agencies and the Personal Social Services," in Powell, *The Nonprofit Sector*, p. 253.
9. Increases in GFO rates in one contracted service pressure the NPA to subsidize, or more heavily subsidize, staff salaries in other programs. A manager explains that one GFO advises him that the state pays $5,000 more a year for a worker with a BA than his NPA pays and that the GFO is prepared to reimburse contracted services staff by that additional amount. This increase, however, will skew this large NPA's entire salary scale. His NPA "must now decide" how to resolve "that kind of conflict" with its "complications."
10. Peter M. Kettner and Lawrence L. Martin, "Purchase of Service Contracting with For-Profit Organizations," *Administration in Social Work* 4 (1988): 47–60.
11. For a discussion of the similarities and differences, see Richard Steinberg, "Nonprofit Organizations and the Market," in Powell, *The Nonprofit Sector*, pp. 118–38.

CHAPTER NINE

PREREQUISITES

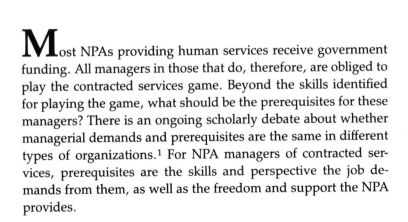

Most NPAs providing human services receive government funding. All managers in those that do, therefore, are obliged to play the contracted services game. Beyond the skills identified for playing the game, what should be the prerequisites for these managers? There is an ongoing scholarly debate about whether managerial demands and prerequisites are the same in different types of organizations.[1] For NPA managers of contracted services, prerequisites are the skills and perspective the job demands from them, as well as the freedom and support the NPA provides.

While the administrative and political challenges of contracted services' management may require extraordinary skills, managers believe the nature of these skills is basic, "not fancy." Their perception is consistent with the "handyman model" of the role of managers, "the one best supported by the few empirical studies of what nonprofit executives actually do."[2] A compliance coordinator says, "I think you need to be a very well organized, rational person with good administrative skills." Another manager catalogues the skills.

> You have to be very well organized. You have to work hard and put in a lot of time on your job. You have to be able to deal with a lot of different kinds of problems from the sublime to the ridiculous, from the more abstract to the more concrete. You have to be able to assimilate a lot of different kinds of rules and regulations—keep them in mind. I think you have to have good techniques and abilities around interviewing and hiring staff because those are crucial decisions. You have to have some ability to get along with people.

A manager who was told to develop a corrective action plan because she did not sign some records conceptualizes a basic skill described by several others: "I have to come up with something that takes a stupid thing seriously." An executive director points out, however, that managers must be able to "appreciate the ramifications" of the legal relationship with the GFO because "it usually only comes to the fore when there's a crisis of some sort and you get accused of not doing something."

Managers include political savvy among the basic skills required for the management of contracted services. A program director says she learned, by "watching" her supervisors, to be "very politically savvy": "I know how to present to our funders the real important, salient issues that make our program attractive, as well as worthy of continuing support." A compliance coordinator gives a graphic description of the importance of her basic political skills.

> There's an old boys' school here among the directors, and there can be a lot of resistance to change. New kids on the block don't get accepted too quick. I really wanted to stay at the agency. I just continued to make them more and more dependent on me in a lot of different areas. I write very well. I have a sense of how things are to operate. If you've never done it, if you've never treated a patient, would you go in and treat a patient? It doesn't come from the books. If you've never held somebody who's crying, what do you know about this? If you've never wiped a kid's runny nose, do you know? It's not because I've had all this training, because I have a doctorate. It's because I can go and I can teach and I can do, and I don't mind getting my hands dirty. And that's my power. In my own way, I have a lot of power.

According to managers, the other prerequisite for what managers must bring to their jobs is a philosophical perspective. They understand the essence of the work; transforming their understanding into action requires a sophisticated balancing act. An executive director says, "I guess you have to have the ability to always juggle X number of things at one time." The "X number of things," though, are not just tasks; they are values and goals and management imperatives.

A compliance coordinator explains the overriding importance of perspective for managers of contracted services.

> I think the most important thing is keeping in perspective what your job is. You could get so caught up in the forms they could overtake you. That could become your whole job—becoming a forms expert—and you lose sight of who the kids are, and the families, and the people who work in the system, and what the system's goal is, and

what the system is responding to in terms of the larger social issues. If you lose sight of all of that, then most likely you're not going to do your job well, is the way I see it.

She then describes how she does not "lose sight of all that."

I think because of my many different roles here, it probably helps. Because I'm admissions, I get that aspect of it—of the people desperately needing to come in here, and what they've been through to get here. Social work students have come and that whole perspective. I think that really does help. Just being willing to listen to people out there, even if they're angry and upset about what I have to do. Being open and hearing what's going on. Also I try and balance out my job and not make it all compliance stuff—I still see some families. I do that for my own sanity because the job can be absurd.

An executive director says he performs the balancing act between good management and his "primary responsibility to the people that we serve" by defining contract compliance as "the best quality of service," not adherence to the letter of the law.

I think that I'm a damn good manager, and I think that we've got on staff excellent managers, but basically the way I've run the agency is that our primary responsibility is to the people that we serve, and if we have to fight our funding agencies, and if we have to stretch things, we do. As long as the money is not going into anybody's pocket, as long as we're providing the best quality of service, as long as we're meeting our contract, I see nothing wrong with it.

A program director believes that social work experience and values make it possible to do the balancing act required to manage contracted services.

> I've learned in my old age, . . . not only do you need ex-
> perience, you need experience as a social worker. I had a
> lot of experience before I went into social work so that's
> why I used to say [that any kind of experience is appro-
> priate], but there's something about being in the field,
> dealing with the values, dealing with what it means to be
> a social worker. I think it does make a difference, and I'm
> not able to articulate it.

A compliance coordinator feels, however, that social work
experience does not "make a difference" because much of the
balancing act involves "common-sense issues."

> I would want a well-organized, compassionate person
> who had a good sense of himself. That would summarize
> it. I don't think it matters if their background is in social
> work or not. I really don't. Maybe I don't give myself
> enough credit, but I think you're dealing with a lot of
> common sense issues, and they're not deep clinical issues
> where you need any kind of advanced clinical training.

She defines "common sense" as being able, for example, to "tell
what's good for a child, as opposed to what's good for a state
department."

Another manager fears "getting so immersed" in daily contract demands that she does not address their validity. The "danger" for her, she says, is "to respond constantly to the specific."
Her goal is "comprehensive care for older people," and she says,
"Whatever that means, within my human possibility I will pursue." Although "it's very, very hard" and she is not always
successful, she explains how she maintains her philosophical
perspective.

> I'm very clear what my goals are and just keep those in-
> side of me. If I didn't have clear direction and goals for
> myself, I would just wander down this path or that path.

Managers must also do a balancing act in reconciling the reality that GFO funding is not commensurate with the magnitude of the problems. A manager describes this struggle.

> When you're working with a homebound, isolated elderly person, you could spend all your time with one client because of the tremendous need, and yet the contractor's saying you must see more people. And how do you live with that? And how do you help workers realize that they may not [spend sufficient time with each client]?

An executive director talks about the "terrible choices" involved in finding a balance when the options for children needing out-of-home care are "an abomination": "You do get caught in trying to avoid the worst, to make the best decision you can in a very bad situation." For many managers, the balance comes by involving themselves in NPA coalitions fighting for increased resources.

In trying to hire someone to do quality assurance, another manager rejects those with master's degrees in public health. Since "every single thing [in hospital administration] becomes life and death," she explains, these applicants are "all so serious." Whereas, given the complexity and intractability of the problems her NPA addresses, "If you don't keep this in perspective, you're a dead duck."

> The perspective is just we cannot save the world. We cannot in this sort of place here. Housing is still a problem. Drugs are still a problem. AIDS is still a problem. We can't prevent that stuff. So I always try and keep in perspective what our goal is here.

Effectively playing the contracted services game requires that managers have basic administrative and political skills and a philosophical perspective. But these are insufficient. There are prerequisites for the management of contracted services that NPAs must satisfy. To enable them to do their jobs, managers need the NPA to provide freedom and support.

Paradoxically, for managers to be effective despite rigid, detailed, and intrusive GFO contractual regulations, they need from the NPA the freedom to function autonomously, to be creative, and to take risks. Asked what difference it would make if her contracted service became a direct GFO program, a manager is stunned but responds without hesitation.

> We'd all quit. It's the [GFO's] system—it's so chaotic. The thought of it even boggles my mind.
>
> First of all, we do have the luxury as a voluntary agency of not having to take every case that comes through the door. The city can't do that. So sheer numbers, I think, make it very tough for the city. We don't have that. I have some control over my destiny and my workers.

Three managers describe what the freedom to function autonomously means to them.

> They don't know what I'm doing half the time. We do our own thing around here. And I don't really want it to be otherwise.

> They really respect and give me the freedom with what I'm doing. More than usual it would be me who would go to them and ask for input than them even commenting on the things that I'm doing.

> Here, I do what I think is necessary. I'm given fairly much free rein. Few people really understand what I do other than I get the job done. We keep getting better [GFO] evaluations. I have nobody really looking over my shoulder.

Managers also prize the freedom to be creative.

I always feel like I'm not doing enough. I think that's the nature of the animal. I feel like my expertise happens to be that I'm much more of a creative thinker probably than a professional kind of manager.

In general, I would think that people would want to be in a private agency rather than government because there's a sense of more control over what they do and how they do it and input into that because they do have more.

Another freedom managers apparently value in the NPA is the freedom to take risks. This is consistent with the empirical research indicating "nonprofit executives almost inevitably put themselves in some kind of jeopardy—financial, professional, legal—if they are to get things done."[3] The willingness to take risks pervades managers' stories.

Their career paths reflect a willingness and desire to seize possible opportunities and take risks. For example, two of the executive directors began working as volunteers with their NPAs. One was recruited by the NPA executive when the two met at a university recruitment fair where they were representing their respective colleges. The executive offered him a ride home. He began volunteer work for the NPA, eventually left his job and took a paid position, and six years later was himself the executive director. The other manager began work for the embryonic NPA as a student, was then employed on a state hospital's janitor line to work for the NPA, and eventually became the executive director. An indication of his ability to seize opportunities is his recruitment of a board member: "I met one guy on a plane."

All the other managers, whether they are new to their NPAs or have worked there for their entire professional careers, are risk takers to some degree. They are the ones the NPA turns to when programs are consolidated, when new programs are added, when change has to be managed. On their own initiative they develop proposals, carve out positions for themselves, and assume leadership in NPA coalition efforts. They risk the unknown and seem to thrive on on-the-job training. And they skillfully play the paradoxical, crazy, hazardous game of contracted services.

After describing how her NPA is going to resolve a "catch-22" GFO requirement by having one program, without GFO authorization and in technical violation of the regulations, serve two populations, she explains:

> I realize the risk but said let's go with it because I really believe it's providing service. It's not going to benefit me—it might make me crazier in the long run.

An executive director explains that he gets a new facility for his NPA by fund-raising in the community—"collecting pennies, literally." Like all risk takers, he cannot wait "till all of the pieces [are] in place."

> We ended up taking out about two hundred thousand dollars in short-term notes—and of that two hundred thousand, at this point now we're one hundred thirty thousand shy—but we've still got three years to raise that money, so I'm confident that we'll do it. It was the kind of thing that if we waited till all of the pieces were in place, we never would have done it, because we would have lost the [building]. They're never all in place. We just had to go ahead and do it. Now we can actually walk potential contributors through it, and they can see what's going on. It makes a lot more sense than just looking at a plan and a brochure.

As much as managers value the freedom they get from the NPA and consider it a prerequisite for management of contracted services, they simultaneously value and consider support to be a prerequisite. Fundamentally, managers value working with people with whom they share a service philosophy, respect, and trust. An executive director says the "most important things" the board should look for in his replacement are "the ability to hire people you can trust and who know what they're doing" and "an understanding of what you're trying to do to begin with so you know if it's going in the right direction." He says "what makes the agency" is "who you've got out there doing the job."

For a compliance coordinator, support means that when she concludes that the NPA will not meet a GFO requirement, her executive director accepts her decision. Another manager explains the significance of the support in his NPA by contrasting it with what he sees in the GFO.

> In general, there's just about no one on the [NPA] staff that I don't respect. I'm tired of walking into [the GFO] and watching people read newspapers. I am tired of watching how [the GFO] scapegoats middle management.

A manager describes what support looks like in her program.

> When we do things for patients, like Christmas parties, we do it like a team. We've really been very lucky. They bring in boyfriends: One staff person's husband was Santa Claus; the other staff's boyfriend was the photographer. I found a friend to come in and do magic tricks. [One person's] husband brings our [financial reports] down to [the GFO]—he's retired—so she doesn't have to go down to [the GFO] everyday. There's a lot of real extra, extra stuff that goes on here.

Managers want freedom, but they want the support of knowing that those to whom they report know what is happening in their programs and are advocates for what they need to function. A manager describes her executive director as "very supportive, hands-on, and connected to his programs." Another manager in a very large NPA describes his department head as "a real advocate for her department." He says, for example, "She's always been able to come up with creative ways to reduce the effects of cutbacks."

One manager explains how she values the support inherent in her NPA's ability to subsidize GFO payment delays.

> I simply do not have to worry about whether we're going to have payroll. I don't think I could do this—I couldn't ask people to work at the salaries that they work at and then worry about whether they're getting paid because jerky bureaucrats can't deposit vouchers. I just couldn't do it.

Repeatedly, managers face crises as they manage contracted services. They make the hard decisions; they take the heat. But they need support from those with whom they work. After explaining what happens after a child in one of the families her program is serving set his house on fire, killing his mother, the manager concludes:

> These are things that make a big difference, to have people who are very, very, very supportive. Also, we do a lot on a management level out of the team. I never feel like I'm alone.

Another manager explains the importance of the support of executive staff colleagues when she mandates compliance with a very unpopular GFO requirement. Without their "unconditional love," she says, "you might as well jump."

One manager explains that despite fighting among NPA staff and their resistance to change, she knows she will have their support if she ever has a personal crisis.

But underneath it all is that if anyone of us in this executive group were in trouble, they're all there. See, they can want to kill you, but they're all there. If there's a family problem, if there's a divorce problem, they're all behind you. And that's the good part of it.

Managers also consider support from an NPA coalition to be a prerequisite for playing the game of contracted services. They use these coalitions to learn the rules, to enter the game, to gain some control over it, and to summon the courage to continue playing. A manager describes what happens at these meetings of her colleagues.

A lot of these issues are discussed, and we share and support and console each other and deal with these things— it's really quite difficult.

NOTES

1. See Michael O'Neill and Dennis R. Young, "Educating Managers of Nonprofit Organizations," in Michael O'Neill and Dennis R. Young, eds., *Educating Managers of Nonprofit Organizations* (New York: Praeger, 1988), pp. 1–21; and Dennis R. Young, "Executive Leadership in Nonprofit Organizations," in Walter W. Powell, ed., *The Nonprofit Sector: A Research Handbook* (New Haven, Conn.: Yale University Press, 1987), pp. 167–79. In the social work administration literature, managerial demands and prerequisites are characterized as distinct. See Charles S. Levy, *Guide to Ethical Decisions and Actions for Social Service Administrators: A Handbook for Managerial Personnel* (New York: The Haworth Press, 1982), p. 72; Simon Slavin, "Different Types of Nonprofit Managers," in O'Neill and Young, *Educating Managers of Nonprofit Organizations*, pp. 83–94; Morton I. Teicher, "Who Should Manage a Social Agency?" in Simon Slavin, ed., *An Introduction to Human Services Management*, vol. 1 of *Social Administration: The Management of the Social Services*, 2d ed. (New York: The Haworth Press, 1985), pp. 44–49; and Rino J. Patti, *Social Welfare Administra-*

tion/*Managing Social Programs in a Developmental Context* (Englewood Cliffs: Prentice-Hall, 1983), pp. 26–27.

2. Paul J. DiMaggio, "Nonprofit Managers in Different Fields of Service: Managerial Tasks and Management Training," in O'Neill and Young, *Educating Managers of Nonprofit Organizations*, pp. 53–55.

3. Young, "Executive Leadership in Nonprofit Organizations," in Powell, *The Nonprofit Sector*, p. 177. Risk taking is inherent in entrepreneurship. For reports of Young's research on entrepreneurship in nonprofit organizations, see ibid., pp. 167–79; Dennis R. Young, *If Not for Profit, for What? A Behavioral Theory of the Nonprofit Sector Based on Entrepreneurship* (Lexington, Mass.: Lexington Books, 1983); and Dennis R. Young, *Casebook of Management for Nonprofit Organizations: Entrepreneurship and Organizational Change in the Human Services* (New York: The Haworth Press, 1985).